KITCHEN
TABLE

100 Weeknight Curries

KITCHEN
TABLE

100 Weeknight Curries
MADHUR JAFFREY

www.mykitchentable.co.uk

Welcome to **my** KITCHEN TABLE

All of the curries in this collection are designed
to be **simple, hassle-free and full of flavour**. With
everything from quick snacks to hearty family meals,
I hope you find something to suit every occasion.

Contents

Summery Yoghurt Soup

A perfect soup for a hot summer's day. You can have all the ingredients ready ahead of time and combine them at the last minute. If you wish to save time, you may omit peeling and seeding the tomatoes and simply dice them.

Step one Boil the new potatoes for 15–20 minutes, until tender, then drain and leave to cool. Peel and cut them into small dice.

Step two Put the oil into a very small pan and set it over medium–high heat. When it is very hot, put in the mustard seeds. As soon as they begin to pop, pour the oil and seeds into a large bowl.

Step three Add the yoghurt to the bowl and beat it lightly with a whisk until smooth and creamy, then slowly whisk in the stock and cream. Then add all the remaining ingredients, including the potatoes, and mix them in with a wooden spoon. Chill until ready to serve.

Serves 4

4 smallish new potatoes, unpeeled

1 tablespoon olive oil

$\frac{1}{2}$ teaspoon brown mustard seeds

600ml (1 pint) natural yoghurt

900ml (1$\frac{1}{2}$ pints) good-quality chicken stock, degreased and strained through a fine sieve

6 tablespoons single cream

8 tablespoons finely diced peeled cucumber

2 tomatoes, peeled, seeded and diced

$\frac{1}{8}$–$\frac{1}{4}$ teaspoon cayenne pepper (depending how hot you like it)

2 teaspoons very finely chopped fresh dill

salt and freshly ground black pepper

Easy Mulligatawny Soup

A wonderful Anglo–Indian soup, this may be served as a first course or as a light lunch. Stir the soup well before serving as all dal soups tend to separate slightly.

Serves 4–6

3 tablespoons olive or groundnut oil

1 teaspoon fresh ginger, finely grated

1 teaspoon crushed garlic

1 teaspoon ground cumin

1 teaspoon ground coriander

1½ teaspoons curry powder

⅛–¼ teaspoon cayenne pepper (depending on how hot you like it)

200g (7oz) skinless, boneless chicken thighs, cut into 1cm (½in) dice

175g (6oz) split red lentils (masoor dal), picked over, washed and drained

1.2 litres (2 pints) chicken stock

1 teaspoon salt, or to taste

1 tablespoon lemon juice

1 tablespoon finely chopped fresh coriander

Step one Heat the oil in a heavy-based pan over medium–high heat. When it is hot, put in the ginger and the garlic and stir-fry for 10 seconds. Add the cumin, coriander, curry powder and cayenne and stir-fry for another 10 seconds, then put in the diced chicken and stir-fry for 30 seconds.

Step two Add the split lentils, chicken stock and salt and bring to the boil. Partly cover the pan, reduce the heat to low and simmer for 45 minutes or until the lentils are very soft.

Step three Add the lemon juice and fresh coriander and stir to mix in well.

Spinach and Okra Soup

The first time I had this soup was in the home of an Indo–Trinidadian. Instead of spinach, my host had used the large leaves of the taro root. This delicious creation may be served as either a first course at dinner or a main dish for lunch. Okra is essential here as it binds the soup together, rather like a New Orleans gumbo. It should be washed and patted dry before cutting.

Step one Put the oil in a large pan and set it over medium–high heat. When the oil is hot, put in the onion, garlic, carrot, green beans and okra. Sauté for 5 minutes.

Step two Now put in the spinach and chillies and cook for another 5 minutes. Pour in the stock, stir and bring to the boil. Cover the pan, reduce the heat to low and simmer gently for 25–30 minutes.

Step three Put the soup in a food processor or blender and blend coarsely or smoothly, as desired. You will need to do this in several batches. Return the soup to the pan. Add the coconut milk and some salt and pepper to taste. Stir well and bring to a simmer. Garnish with a few thin slices of okra and serve.

Serves 4–6

4 tablespoons olive or groundnut oil

1 onion, coarsely chopped

3 garlic cloves, coarsely chopped

1 small carrot, cut into coarse rounds

10 green beans, cut into 2.5cm (1in) pieces

7 okra, 6 trimmed and cut crossways into coarse slices, 1 very thinly sliced, to garnish

450g (1lb) fresh spinach, well washed and cut crossways into strips 1cm (½in) wide

1–2 fresh hot green chillies, coarsely sliced

750ml (1¼ pints) chicken stock

400ml (14fl oz) tin coconut milk, well stirred

salt and freshly ground black pepper

Green Soup

This is India's version of cream of pea soup. It is delicate and quite delicious.

Serves 5–6

900g (2lb) potatoes, peeled and roughly diced

75g (3oz) onions, coarsely chopped

1.2 litres (2 pints) chicken stock

2cm (¾in) cube fresh ginger

½ teaspoon ground coriander

2 teaspoons ground cumin

5 tablespoons chopped fresh coriander

½ fresh hot green chilli

275g (10oz) peas, either frozen and defrosted under warm running water, or fresh

¾ teaspoon salt

1 tablespoon lemon juice

½ teaspoon ground, roasted cumin seeds

150ml (¼ pint) double cream

Small fresh hot green chilli, very thinly sliced, to garnish

Step one In a pan, combine the potatoes, onions, chicken stock, ginger, ground coriander and ground cumin and bring to a boil. Cover, turn the heat to low and simmer for 30 minutes.

Step two Fish out the cube of ginger and discard it. Add the coriander, chilli, peas, salt (use a little extra if the stock is unsalted), lemon juice and cumin seeds. Bring to the boil and simmer, uncovered, for 2–3 minutes or until the peas are just tender.

Step three Blend the soup until smooth, in batches if necessary. Add the cream and heat through to a gentle simmer. Serve in bowls garnished with a few slices of fresh hot green chilli.

Fried Pappadums

Pappadums have been part of Indian meals since ancient times, adding both a crunchy texture and nutritional value to the humblest of repasts. The ones you buy 'raw' are actually partly prepared. The manufacturers start with a split pea dough, which they can leave plain or flavour with black pepper, chillies or garlic. They make small patties out of the dough and roll them out into thin discs, rather like chapatis. These discs are dried in the sun but they still need to be roasted or fried. Here is the frying method.

Serves 6

groundnut oil, for deep-frying

6 pappadums

Step one Pour some oil into a large frying pan to a depth of 2cm (¾in) and set it over medium heat. When the oil is very hot, put in a pappadum (or half a pappadum, depending upon size). It will sizzle and expand in seconds.

Step two Remove the pappadum with a slotted spoon and drain on kitchen paper. Cook the remaining pappadums in the same way.

Pappadums expand during frying, so make sure you allow plenty of room in the pan.

Spicy Cashews

There is nothing as good as freshly fried cashews. My mother always made them for my father, to accompany his evening drink during the winter months. After frying, she would let them drain briefly on thick brown paper, from the same batch she used to cover all our books, and then she served them in bowls made out of coconut shells. She just sprinkled salt and black pepper on them but I add a little cayenne pepper as well. The frying oil may be reused.

Serves 4–6

olive, vegetable or groundnut oil, for deep-frying

225g (8oz) raw cashew nuts

¼ teaspoon salt

⅛ teaspoon cayenne pepper

freshly ground black pepper

Step one Put a sieve on top of a metal bowl and set aside. Pour some oil into a deep frying pan to a depth of about 2.5cm (1in) and set it over medium heat. When the oil is very hot, put in all the cashews. Stir and fry until they turn a reddish-gold colour (this happens quite fast).

Step two Empty the contents of the frying pan into the sieve to drain off the oil, then scatter the cashews over a baking tray lined with kitchen paper.

Step three Sprinkle the salt, cayenne and some black pepper over the cashews while they are still hot and mix well. Serve warm or at room temperature.

For more recipes from My Kitchen Table, sign up for our newsletter at www.mykitchentable.co.uk/newsletter

Potato Bhajias

Both the potatoes and their skins are used in these bhajias. Great for snacking and, as a first course, they are generally served with chutney, such as the Fresh Green Chutney (see page 188) or with tomato ketchup.

Step one To make the batter, sift the flour, bicarbonate of soda, spices and salt into a large bowl. Add the cumin seeds, then gradually pour in about 250ml (8fl oz) water, stirring as you go, to make a smooth batter.

Step two Peel the potatoes. Cut the skins into long slices 5mm (¼in) thick, and then cut the peeled potatoes into rounds, 5mm (¼in) thick. Drop the potato pieces – skins and rounds – into the batter and stir to coat them well.

Step three Pour some oil into a karhai, wok or deep frying pan to a depth of 5cm (2in) and set it over low–medium heat. When hot – it should reach 180°C (350°F) if you have a thermometer – take as many potato pieces as will fit in a single layer and scatter them evenly in the hot oil. Fry the potatoes, stirring them occasionally, for about 7 minutes, or until they are golden on both sides. Remove the bhajias with a slotted spoon and spread them out to drain on a large plate lined with kitchen paper. Repeat with the remaining potato pieces and serve hot.

Serves 4–6

for the batter

100g (4oz) chickpea (gram or besan) flour

¼ teaspoon bicarbonate of soda

½ teaspoon ground turmeric

½ teaspoon cayenne pepper

½ teaspoon ground coriander

¾ teaspoon salt

1 teaspoon cumin seeds

for the potatoes

2 potatoes, unpeeled, well scrubbed

groundnut oil, for deep-frying

Hard-boiled Eggs in a Rich Moghlai Sauce

This can be whipped up quite quickly. Here the sauce for the eggs is rich and creamy – hence the 'Moghlai' in the title (in other words, in the style of the Moghlai court). Serve with rice or any bread. I even love these eggs with toast.

Serves 4

½ teaspoon cayenne pepper

1 teaspoon ground cumin

½ teaspoon garam masala

1 teaspoon ground coriander

1 tablespoon lemon juice

½–¾ teaspoon salt

freshly ground black pepper

2 tablespoons olive or groundnut oil

50g (2oz) onion, finely chopped

2.5cm (1in) piece fresh ginger, grated to a pulp

2 teaspoons tomato purée

150ml (¼ pint) chicken stock

300ml (½ pint) single cream

2 tablespoons chopped fresh coriander, plus a few whole leaves, to garnish

6–8 hard-boiled eggs, peeled and cut lengthways in half

Step one Mix the cayenne, cumin, garam masala, coriander, lemon juice, salt and some black pepper with 1 tablespoon of water in a cup. Set aside.

Step two Put the oil in a large frying pan and set it over medium–high heat. When the oil is hot, add the onion and stir-fry until it turns brown at the edges. Add the ginger and stir for 10 seconds, then add the paste from the cup and stir for 30 seconds. Stir in the tomato purée, chicken stock, cream and fresh coriander and bring to a simmer. Cover and simmer gently for 2–3 minutes.

Step three Lay the egg halves in the sauce in a single layer and spoon the sauce over the top. Cover and simmer very gently for another 2–3 minutes, then serve garnished with whole coriander leaves.

Vinegared Eggs

This vinegary, hard-boiled egg dish is almost like a pickle, and it's perfect for taking out on picnics. It is, like all Goan-style vindaloo dishes, tart, hot, garlicky and just very slightly sweet. I have lessened the tartness somewhat by cooking the eggs in a mixture of vinegar and water instead of just vinegar. Use the mildest vinegar that you can find. In this recipe, you may use anywhere from six to eight eggs without having to alter any of the other ingredients. You could serve this dish with rice or an Indian bread.

Step one Mash the garlic cloves to a pulp or put them through a garlic press. Combine the garlic mash, grated ginger, cayenne, paprika, cumin, salt, brown sugar and 2 tablespoons of vinegar in a cup or small bowl. Mix well.

Step two Put the oil in a medium frying pan and set over medium heat. When the oil is hot, put in the cinnamon stick and let it sizzle for a few seconds. Add the onions, then stir-fry for about 5 minutes or until the onions have softened. Add the garlic paste and the garam masala, then stir-fry for 2 minutes.

Step three Add 150ml (¼ pint) vinegar and the water, stir well and bring to a simmer. Put all the egg halves into the frying pan in a single layer, cut-side up, and spoon the sauce over them. Cook on medium heat for about 5 minutes or until the sauce has thickened, spooning the sauce frequently over the eggs as you do so. Remove the cinnamon stick before serving.

Serves 3–4

4 garlic cloves

2.5cm (1in) cube fresh ginger, very finely grated

¼–½ teaspoon cayenne pepper

2 teaspoons paprika

1½ teaspoons ground cumin

1¼ teaspoons salt

1½ tablespoons brown sugar

2 tablespoons mild white vinegar, plus 150ml (¼ pint)

3 tablespoons vegetable oil

2.5cm (1in) stick cinnamon

225g (8oz) onions, finely chopped

½ teaspoon garam masala

175ml (6fl oz) water

6–8 hard-boiled eggs, peeled and halved crossways

23

Hard-boiled Eggs in a Spicy Cream Sauce

This delicious egg dish can be put together quickly and is also perfect for brunches and light lunches. You could serve toast on the side or rice and a crisp salad. For a more traditional Indian meal, parathas or Spiced Basmati Rice (see page 171) would be suitable accompaniments. This recipe calls for a small amount of chicken stock. If you have some home-made stock handy, well and good. Otherwise, use a stock cube.

Serves 3–4

3 tablespoons vegetable oil

50g (2oz) onion, finely chopped

2.5cm (1in) cube fresh ginger, finely grated

½–1 fresh hot green chilli, finely chopped

300ml (½ pint) single cream

1 tablespoon lemon juice

1 teaspoon ground, roasted cumin seeds

¼ teaspoon cayenne pepper

½ teaspoon salt

¼ teaspoon garam masala

2 teaspoons tomato purée

150ml (¼ pint) chicken stock

6–8 hard-boiled eggs

1 tablespoon finely chopped fresh coriander or parsley (optional)

Step one Put the oil in a large non-stick, frying pan and set over medium heat. When hot, put in the onion, then stir-fry for about 3 minutes or until the pieces are browned at the edges. Add the grated ginger and chilli, and stir-fry for a minute. Now add the cream, lemon juice, ground, roasted cumin seeds, cayenne, salt, garam masala, tomato purée and chicken stock. Stir to mix thoroughly and bring to a simmer.

Step two Peel the hard-boiled eggs and halve them crossways. Then add the egg halves to the sauce in a single layer, cut-side up, and spoon the sauce over them. Cook over medium heat for about 5 minutes, spooning the sauce frequently over the eggs as you do so. By this time the sauce will have become fairly thick.

Step three Place the egg halves carefully in a serving dish, cut-side up, and pour the sauce over them. Garnish with fresh coriander or parsley, if you wish, sprinkled lightly over the top.

If you are using a stock cube instead of home-made stock, reduce the amount of salt you add in step one.

Chicken Tikka Masala

To make this recipe, you first have to make Tandoori-style Chicken (see page 79) and then enfold it in a traditional curry sauce. In restaurants, it all tends to look rather red because of the food colouring. Here is my healthier version. When making the Tandoori-style chicken remember to save the marinade and the cooking juices, as you will need them here.

Step one Put the oil into a large, wide pan and set it over a medium–high heat. When the oil is very hot, put in the cardamom pods and cinnamon stick. Stir once, then add the onions. Stir until they begin to turn brown at the edges. Add the ginger and garlic and cook, stirring, for 1 minute. Add the cumin, coriander, turmeric, cayenne and paprika and stir for 30 seconds.

Step two Add the tandoori chicken marinade, a tablespoon at a time, and stir it in so that it is absorbed by the spices.

Step three Add the tomato, tomato purée and garam masala. Cook, stirring continuously, for a minute. Pour in the water and bring to a simmer. Cover, turn the heat to low and simmer gently for 10 minutes. Taste for salt, adding about ¼ teaspoon or as needed.

Step four Add the cooked chicken and the juices from the baking tray. Raise the heat to high and fold the chicken into the sauce. The sauce should thicken and cling to the chicken pieces. Remove the cinnamon stick before serving.

Serves 4

5 tablespoons olive oil

5 cardamom pods

5cm (2in) stick cinnamon

2 onions, finely chopped

2 teaspoons finely grated fresh ginger

2 teaspoons crushed garlic

1 teaspoon each ground cumin and ground coriander

¼ teaspoon ground turmeric

½–1 teaspoon cayenne pepper, to taste

1 tablespoon paprika

4 tablespoons reserved Tandoori-style Chicken marinade

1 large tomato, very finely chopped

1 teaspoon tomato purée

1 teaspoon garam masala

150ml (¼ pint) water

¼ teaspoon salt

1 quantity of Tandoori-style Chicken

27

Creamy Chicken Korma with Almonds

I happen to like dark chicken meat so, given a choice, I would use only chicken thighs for this recipe. However, many people prefer light meat. Whatever chicken pieces you choose, legs must be cut into two parts (drumstick and thigh) and breasts must be cut in half across the centre. If you prefer, you could use a whole chicken, cut into pieces and skinned.

Serves 4

1.5kg (3lb)
chicken pieces

5–6 garlic cloves,
coarsely chopped

2.5cm (1in) piece
fresh ginger, peeled
and chopped

50g (2oz)
flaked almonds

5 tablespoons olive
or groundnut oil

2 bay leaves

8 cardamom pods

4 cloves

2.5cm (1in) stick
cinnamon

1 onion, finely
chopped

1 tablespoon
ground cumin

1 tablespoon
ground coriander

¼ teaspoon
cayenne pepper

1 tablespoon
tomato purée

1¼ teaspoons salt

3 tablespoons
single cream

½ tablespoon
garam masala

Step one Skin the chicken pieces, cut them into serving portions (see above) and set aside. Put the garlic, ginger, almonds and 6 tablespoons water into a blender and blend to a smooth paste. Put the oil in a wide pan and set it over medium–high heat. When the oil is very hot, put in the bay leaves, cardamom pods, cloves and cinnamon stick and stir for 10 seconds. Add the onion and cook, stirring, until browned.

Step two Reduce the heat to medium and add the paste from the blender, along with the cumin, coriander and cayenne. Stir for 3–4 minutes, then add the tomato purée and stir for a minute longer.

Step three Add the chicken pieces, salt, cream, garam masala and 150ml (¼ pint) water. Bring to a simmer, then cover the pan, turn the heat to low and simmer gently for 25 minutes, until the chicken is done. Remove the cinnamon stick and bay leaves just before serving.

Mughlai Chicken with Almonds and Sultanas

This elegant dish could be accompanied by Spiced Basmati Rice (see page 171) and Yoghurt with Walnuts and Fresh Coriander (see page 195).

Step one Put the ginger, garlic, 4 tablespoons of the almonds and 4 tablespoons water into a blender and process to a paste.

Step two Put the oil in a wide non-stick pan on medium–high heat. When the oil is hot brown the chicken pieces, in batches if necessary. Remove with a slotted spoon and set aside.

Step three Put the cardamom pods, cinnamon, bay leaves and cloves into the same hot oil. Stir-fry for a few seconds and then add the onions. Stir-fry to brown them lightly. Add the paste and the cumin and cayenne. Stir-fry for 2–3 minutes or until the oil seems to separate and the spices are lightly browned.

Step four Add 1 tablespoon of the yoghurt, and stir-fry for about 30 seconds. Now add another tablespoon and stir-fry in the same way until all the yoghurt has been used up.

Step five Now add the chicken pieces, and any liquid from the chicken bowl, as well as the cream and salt. Bring to a simmer. Cover, turn the heat to low and cook gently for 20 minutes.

Step six Add the sultanas and turn over the chicken pieces. Cover and cook for a further 10 minutes or until the chicken is tender. Add the garam masala and stir. Remove the cinnamon stick and the bay leaves.

Step seven Scatter the remaining almonds on a baking tray and put them under the grill until they brown lightly. You have to toss them frequently to avoid them burning. Sprinkle these almonds over the chicken to serve. Any fat floating on the top of the dish can be spooned off just before serving.

Serves 6

2.5cm (1in) cube fresh ginger, peeled and chopped

8–9 garlic cloves

6 tablespoons blanched, slivered almonds

7 tablespoons vegetable oil

1.5kg (3lb) chicken pieces, skinned

10 cardamom pods

2.5cm (1in) stick cinnamon

2 bay leaves

5 cloves

200g (7oz) onions, finely chopped

2 teaspoons ground cumin

¼–½ teaspoon cayenne pepper

7 tablespoons natural yoghurt

300ml (½ pint) single cream

1½ teaspoons salt

1–2 tablespoons sultanas

¼ teaspoon garam masala

Egg Curry

This is one of my favourite egg curries. It is hot and spicy and quite typical of Malaysian food.

Serves 6–8

2–15 dried hot red chillies, crumbled

½ teaspoon black peppercorns

1 tablespoon coriander seeds

2 sticks lemon grass, finely sliced

4cm (1½in) cube fresh galangal, chopped

4cm (1½in) cube fresh ginger, peeled and chopped

3 teaspoons ground turmeric

18 eggs

9 tablespoons vegetable oil

100g (4oz) shallots or onions, finely sliced

2 garlic cloves, chopped

1 litre (1¾ pints) coconut milk

3 tablespoons tamarind paste, or 2 tablespoons lime juice

2½ teaspoons salt

1 teaspoon sugar

275g (10oz) tomatoes, cut into 2.5cm (1in) dice

4 each fresh hot green and red chillies

fresh mint sprigs

Step one Place the dried chillies, peppercorns, coriander seeds, sliced lemon grass, galangal, ginger and turmeric in a blender and add 2 tablespoons water. Process thoroughly. Add another few tablespoons of water if needed to make a paste.

Step two Place the eggs in a large pan, cover well with water and bring to the boil. Reduce the heat to low and simmer for about 12 minutes until the eggs are hard-boiled. Peel under cold running water.

Step three Put the oil in a wide non-stick pan over medium–high heat. When the oil is hot add the shallots or onions and garlic and stir-fry until golden. Add the paste from the blender and stir-fry for 10 minutes or until the oil separates and the paste darkens. Stir in the coconut milk, then add the tamarind paste or lime juice, salt and sugar. Mix well.

Step four Bring to a simmer while stirring and, as soon as the sauce begins to bubble, turn off the heat. Strain through a sieve, pushing through as much liquid as possible. Return the sauce to the pan and add the eggs. (This much of the dish can be prepared a day ahead and chilled.)

Step five Just before serving, bring the curry to a simmer, add the tomatoes and stir a few times, then transfer to a serving dish and top with chillies and mint.

The fresh chillies give the dish a Malaysian look but you can use slivers cut from fresh red and green pepper, if you prefer.

Hearty Chicken Curry with Potatoes

This curry from Kuala Lumpur is extra spicy and rich. It is delicious served with bread – from French or Italian loaves to pittas and chapatis – or with rice. It can easily be made a day in advance and kept in the fridge.

Step one Place the cardamom pods, cloves, star anise, cinnamon stick, fennel seeds and cumin in a clean coffee grinder or spice grinder, then grind as finely as possible. Transfer to a bowl. Add the ground coriander, chilli powder, paprika and 8 tablespoons water, and mix to a thick paste.

Step two Put the ginger, garlic, the three chopped onions and 4 tablespoons water in a blender. Process to a smooth paste.

Step three Divide the chicken legs into thighs and drumsticks. If using breasts, cut in half. Heat the oil in a large, wide pan, add the sliced onion and stir-fry until golden brown. Stir in the paste from the blender and the spice paste from the bowl. Stir-fry for 10–12 minutes until the mixture is well fried and dark.

Step 4 Add 700ml (1¼ pints) water, the chicken, drained potatoes and salt, and bring to a simmer. Cover, reduce the heat and cook gently for 30 minutes or until the chicken is tender. Give the coconut milk a good stir and then pour it into the pan. Cook for a further minute, then add the mint leaves. Fish out the cinnamon sticks and remove the oil floating on top of the curry before serving.

Use less than the recommend quantity of chilli powder if you prefer a mild curry.

Serves 6

6–8 cardamom pods

6 cloves

2 star anise

2 x 5cm (2in) sticks cinnamon

2 tablespoons fennel seeds

1½ tablespoons cumin seeds

4 tablespoons ground coriander

1½–2 teaspoons chilli powder, or to taste

1 tablespoon paprika

4 x 2.5cm (1in) cubes fresh ginger, peeled and chopped

1 tablespoon chopped garlic

4 onions, 3 chopped and 1 finely sliced

1.75kg (4lb) chicken pieces, preferably legs, skinned

175ml (6fl oz) vegetable oil

450g (1lb) potatoes, cut into 2.5cm (1in) cubes and left in water

1 tablespoon salt

200ml (7fl oz) tinned coconut milk

handful fresh mint leaves, chopped

KITCHEN TABLE

For a video masterclass on how to chop an onion, go to
www.mykitchentable.co.uk/videos/choppingonion

Hard-boiled Eggs Cooked with Potatoes

This simple dish is a family favourite. We eat it with an Indian bread or plain rice. It makes a pleasant change from meat, and is economical, too.

Serves 2–4

2 garlic cloves

2.5cm (1in) cube fresh ginger, peeled and chopped

450g (1lb) potatoes, peeled

6 tablespoons vegetable oil

150g (5oz) onions, finely chopped

¼ teaspoon cayenne pepper

1 tablespoon ground coriander

1 teaspoon plain flour

4 tablespoons natural yoghurt

300g (11oz) tomatoes, peeled and finely chopped

1½ teaspoons salt

½ teaspoon garam masala

1 tablespoon very finely chopped fresh coriander or parsley

4 hard-boiled eggs, peeled

Step one Put the garlic, ginger and 2 tablespoons water into a food processor or blender and process to a paste. Cut the potatoes into 1cm (½in) thick slices. Now cut the slices lengthways into 1cm (½in) wide chips.

Step two Put the oil in a large non-stick frying pan and set over medium–high heat. When the oil is hot, put in the potatoes. Turn and fry them until all sides are golden brown. The potatoes should not cook through. Remove them with a slotted spoon and set aside on a plate.

Step three Put the onions into the same oil. Stir-fry until they turn medium brown. Add the garlic–ginger paste and stir-fry for a minute. Add the cayenne, ground coriander and flour and stir for a minute. Put in 1 tablespoon of the yoghurt and stir for about 30 seconds or until it has been incorporated into the sauce. Add all the yoghurt this way, 1 tablespoon at a time. Now put in the tomatoes and stir-fry for 2 minutes. Add 300ml (½ pint) water and the salt. Bring to a boil, cover, reduce the heat to low and simmer for 10 minutes.

Step four Put the potatoes into the sauce and bring to a simmer. Cover, turn the heat to low and simmer for 10 minutes or until the potatoes are just tender.

Step five Add the garam masala and fresh coriander or parsley and stir gently. Halve the eggs crossways and carefully put them into the frying pan with the cut sides up. Try not to let the yolks fall out. Spoon some sauce over the eggs and bring to a simmer. Cover and simmer on low heat for 5 minutes, then serve while still hot.

Goan-style Chicken with Roasted Coconut

I just love this dish. I ate it for the first time in balmy, palm-fringed, coastal Goa, and have been hoarding the recipe ever since. Even though there are several steps to the recipe, it is not at all hard to put together. You could serve this dish with Spicy Green Beans (see page 147).

Step one Into a small, preferably cast-iron, frying pan put the coriander seeds, cumin seeds, mustard seeds, cinnamon, cloves, peppercorns, nutmeg and red chilli. Place the pan over medium heat. Now quickly dry-roast the spices, stirring frequently until they emit a very pleasant 'roasted' aroma. Empty the spices into a clean coffee grinder or spice grinder and grind until fine, then place in a bowl.

Step two Put the coconut into the same frying pan and dry-roast it over medium heat, stirring it continuously. The coconut should pick up lots of brown flecks and also smell 'roasted'. Add to the dry-roasted spices.

Step three Put the garlic, ginger and green chilli into a blender along with 4 tablespoons water. Process to a paste.

Step four Put the oil in a 25–30cm (10–12in) frying pan over medium–high heat. When the oil is hot, put in the onions and cook until they pick up brown spots. Now pour in the garlic–ginger mixture from the blender and stir once. Lower the heat to medium. Put in the chicken pieces, salt and the spice–coconut mixture. Stir-fry the chicken for 3–4 minutes or until it loses its pinkness and turns slightly brown.

Step five Add 300ml (½ pint) water and bring to a simmer. Cover the pan tightly, reduce the heat to low, and cook for 25–30 minutes or until the chicken is tender. Stir a few times during cooking, turning over each piece of chicken so that it colours evenly. Fish out the cinnamon pieces before serving.

Serves 4–5

1½ tablespoons coriander seeds

1½ teaspoons cumin seeds

1 teaspoon black mustard seeds

2.5cm (1in) stick cinnamon, broken into 3–4 pieces

4 cloves

¼ teaspoon black peppercorns

about ⅛ nutmeg

1 dried hot red chilli (seeded if you want it mild)

grated fresh coconut measured to the 450ml (¾ pint) level in a measuring jug

6–8 garlic cloves

2.5cm (1in) cube fresh ginger, peeled and chopped

½–1 fresh hot green chilli

4 tablespoons vegetable oil

175g (6oz) onions, minced

1kg (2¼lb) chicken pieces, skinned

1½ teaspoons salt

Chicken in a Butter Sauce

The sauce in this dish should be folded into the butter at the very last minute as it tends to separate otherwise. However, you can combine all the ingredients, except the butter, up to a day ahead of time and refrigerate them until they are needed. This is a wonderfully simple but spectacular dish in which the Tandoori-style Chicken (see page 79) is transformed with a sauce.

Serves 4–6

for the sauce

4 tablespoons
tomato purée

2.5cm (1in) cube fresh
ginger, peeled and
grated very finely to
a pulp

300ml (½ pint)
single cream

1 teaspoon
garam masala

¾ teaspoon salt

¼ teaspoon sugar

1 fresh hot green chilli,
finely chopped

¼ teaspoon
cayenne pepper

1 tablespoon
very finely chopped
fresh coriander

4 teaspoons
lemon juice

1 teaspoon ground,
roasted cumin seeds

for the chicken

100g (4oz)
unsalted butter

1 quantity of Tandoori-
style Chicken

Step one First prepare the sauce. Put the tomato purée in a large clear measuring jug. Slowly add water, mixing as you go, to make up 250ml (8fl oz) of tomato sauce. Add the remaining sauce ingredients and mix well.

Step two Heat the butter in a wide sauté pan or a large frying pan. When the butter has melted, add the spiced sauce. Bring to a simmer and cook on medium heat for a minute, mixing in the butter as you do so. Add the chicken pieces (but not their accumulated juices). Stir once and put the chicken pieces on a warm serving platter. Any extra sauce should be spooned over the top.

Lemony Chicken with Fresh Coriander

Here is a delightful lemony, gingery dish that requires quite a lot of fresh coriander. I generally serve it with Spiced Basmati Rice (see page 171).

Step one Put the ginger and 4 tablespoons water into a blender and process to a paste.

Step two Put the oil in a wide, heavy non-stick pan over medium–high heat. When the oil is hot, put in as many chicken pieces as the pan will hold in a single layer and brown on both sides. Remove the chicken pieces with a slotted spoon and put them in a bowl. Brown all the chicken pieces this way.

Step three Put the chopped garlic into the same hot oil. As soon as it turns a medium-brown colour, turn the heat to medium and pour in the paste from the blender. Stir-fry it for a minute. Now add the fresh coriander, chilli, cayenne, ground cumin, ground coriander, turmeric and salt. Stir and cook for a minute.

Step four Add all the chicken pieces to the pan, as well as any liquid that might have accumulated in the chicken bowl, along with 150ml (¼ pint) water and the lemon juice. Stir and bring to a boil. Cover the pan tightly, reduce the heat to low and cook for 15 minutes.

Step five Turn the chicken pieces over. Cover again and cook for a further 10–15 minutes or until the chicken is tender. If the sauce is too thin, uncover the pan and boil some of it away over slightly higher heat.

Serves 6

2 x 2.5cm (1in) cubes fresh ginger, peeled and chopped

6 tablespoons vegetable oil

1.25kg (2½lb) chicken pieces, skinned

5 garlic cloves, very finely chopped

200g (7oz) fresh coriander, very finely chopped

½–1 fresh hot green chilli, very finely chopped

¼ teaspoon cayenne pepper

2 teaspoons ground cumin

1 teaspoon ground coriander

½ teaspoon ground turmeric

1 teaspoon salt, or to taste

2 tablespoons lemon juice

Chicken with Tomatoes and Garam Masala

This simple chicken dish used to be a great favourite with our children. This is delicious served with Plain Basmati Rice (see page 164).

Serves 6

5 tablespoons vegetable oil

¾ teaspoon cumin seeds

2.5cm (1in) stick cinnamon

6 cardamom pods

2 bay leaves

¼ teaspoon peppercorns

175g (6oz) onions, finely chopped

6–7 garlic cloves, finely chopped

2.5cm (1in) cube fresh ginger, peeled and finely chopped

450g (1lb) tomatoes or tinned tomatoes, peeled and finely chopped

1.5kg (3lb) chicken pieces, skinned

1½ teaspoons salt

¼–½ teaspoon cayenne pepper

½ teaspoon garam masala

Step one Put the oil in a large, wide pan and set over medium–high heat. When the oil is hot, put in the cumin seeds, cinnamon, cardamom pods, bay leaves and peppercorns. Stir once and then add the onions, garlic and ginger. Stir this mixture around until the onions pick up brown specks.

Step two Add the tomatoes to the pan, along with the chicken pieces, salt and cayenne pepper. Stir to mix and bring to a boil. Cover tightly, reduce the heat to low and simmer for 25 minutes or until the chicken is tender. Stir a few times during cooking.

Step three Remove the cover and increase the heat to medium. Sprinkle in the garam masala and cook, stirring gently, for about 5 minutes in order to reduce the liquid in the pan somewhat. Remove the cinnamon stick and bay leaves before serving.

Chicken in a Sweet Red Pepper Sauce

Many of the traditional meat, poultry and fish dishes served along India's west coast have thick, stunningly red sauces. The main ingredient, which provides both the texture and the colour, is red chillies – fresh or dried. It is almost impossible to find the correct variety of bright red and just mildly hot chilli in the West, but a combination of red peppers and cayenne pepper works exceedingly well! I like to serve this dish with Aromatic Yellow Rice (see page 168) and Yoghurt with Aubergines (see page 191).

Step one If the chicken legs are whole, divide the drumsticks from the thighs with a knife. Breasts should be cut into four parts. Set aside until needed.

Step two Put the onions, ginger, garlic, almonds, red peppers, cumin, coriander, turmeric, cayenne and salt into a food processor or blender. Process to a paste, pushing down with a rubber spatula whenever you need to.

Step three Put the oil in a large, wide non-stick pan and set over medium–high heat. When the oil is hot, pour in all the paste. Stir-fry for 10–12 minutes or until you see the oil forming tiny bubbles around the paste.

Step four Add the chicken to the pan, along with 250ml (8fl oz) water, the lemon juice and the black pepper. Stir to mix and bring to the boil. Cover, reduce the heat to low and simmer gently for 25 minutes or until the chicken is tender. Stir a few times during cooking. Garnish the chicken with sprigs of mint.

Serves 4

1kg (2¼ lb) chicken pieces, skinned

100g (4oz) onions, chopped

2.5cm (1in) cube fresh ginger, peeled and chopped

3 garlic cloves

25g (1oz) blanched, slivered almonds

350g (12oz) red pepper, seeded and coarsely chopped

1 tablespoon ground cumin

2 teaspoons ground coriander

½ teaspoon ground turmeric

¼ –½ teaspoon cayenne pepper

2 teaspoons salt

7 tablespoons vegetable oil

2 tablespoons lemon juice

½ teaspoon coarsely ground black pepper

mint sprigs, to garnish

For a video masterclass on knife skills, go to www.mykitchentable.co.uk/videos/knifeskills

KITCHEN TABLE

Chicken Curry, Lombok-style

In Indonesia, the sauce for this dish is made with fresh, hot chillies, which are slim and long. I use sweet red pepper and chillies to calm the heat.

Serves 4–6

1 red pepper, seeded and coarsely chopped

3 fresh long, hot red chillies, chopped

2.5cm (1in) cube fresh ginger, peeled and chopped

2.5cm (1in) piece fresh galangal, chopped

3 candlenuts or 6 cashew nuts

8 shallots or 1 large onion, chopped

4–5 garlic cloves

½ teaspoon shrimp paste (terasi) or anchovy paste

¼ teaspoon cumin seeds

1 teaspoon black peppercorns

4 cloves

2.5cm (1in) stick cinnamon

400g (14oz) tin coconut milk, unshaken

8 tablespoons vegetable oil

1.5kg (3lb) chicken thighs, or a cut-up chicken

1½ teaspoons salt

1–2 fresh hot red and/or green chillies to garnish (optional)

Step one Into a blender put the red pepper, the red chillies, ginger, galangal, nuts, shallots, garlic and shrimp paste. Process to a smooth paste, adding a little water only if needed.

Step two Put the cumin seeds, peppercorns, cloves and cinnamon into a clean coffee grinder or other spice grinder and grind until fine. Add the ground spices to the paste in the blender and whirr for a few seconds to mix.

Step three Open the can of coconut milk without shaking it. Spoon off the cream at the top and set aside. Pour the remaining milk into a measuring jug and add enough water to make 350ml (12fl oz).

Step four Heat the oil in a wok or a wide non-stick pan over medium–high heat. When the oil is hot, put in the curry paste from the blender. Stir-fry for 6–8 minutes or until the paste is dark red and quite reduced.

Step five Add the chicken pieces and salt to the pan, stir and continue cooking for 2 minutes. Add the thinned coconut milk and bring to the boil. Cover, reduce the heat and simmer gently for 30 minutes.

Step six Uncover the pan and cook on medium heat for 5 minutes. Turn the heat off.

Step seven Spoon off most of the oil. Stir in the reserved coconut cream and mix well. Heat through gently, remove the cinnamon stick and garnish with the additional chillies, if using.

The paste may be made ahead of time and frozen. Defrost thoroughly before using.

Easy Beef Curry

In this curry from Thailand, I use beef skirt, which is such a tender cut of meat it requires hardly any cooking at all. I only stand at the cooker for 12 minutes. Eight minutes are spent frying the spices, and the other four cooking the beef. This is perfect for a small dinner party.

Step one Cut the beef against the grain into pieces 5–7.5cm (2–3in) long, 2.5cm (1in) wide and 3mm ($\frac{1}{8}$in) thick. If you have bought the meat in a long, thin continuous piece, cut it into 7.5cm (3in) segments, then cut each segment against the grain, holding the knife diagonally to the work surface. This will give the required width.

Step two Into a blender put the red pepper, onions, garlic, shrimp paste or anchovy paste and chilli powder. Process until smooth, adding a tablespoon or so of water only if it is needed.

Step three Heat the oil in a wide, shallow pan or frying pan. When the oil is hot, add the spice paste and stir-fry for 7–8 minutes or until the paste turns dark and separates from the oil.

Step four Add the meat and the fish sauce or diluted sweetened soy sauce, stir and cook for 2 minutes. Stir in the coconut milk, then add the salt, kaffir lime leaves, basil and mint. Stir and heat through, then serve.

Kaffir lime leaves have a very distinctive appearance, like a figure of eight with two leaves joined together, base to tip. Any leftover leaves can be stored in a plastic bag in the freezer. They are available dried at Far Eastern and Chinese grocers.

Serves 4

450g beef skirt

125–150g (4½–5oz) seeded, chopped red peppers

100g (4oz) red onions, chopped

garlic

1 teaspoon shrimp paste (terasi) or anchovy paste

¼ teaspoon chilli powder

8 tablespoons vegetable oil

2 tablespoons fish sauce, or 1 tablespoon soy sauce mixed with 1 tablespoon water and ¼ teaspoon sugar

250ml (8fl oz) tinned coconut milk, well stirred

½ teaspoon salt

4 fresh kaffir lime leaves, centre vein removed, or dried kaffir lime leaves (see tip)

10–15 fresh basil leaves, torn

10–15 fresh mint leaves, torn

Lamb, Pork or Beef Madras

In the UK, Madras has come to mean a very hot curry and not much more. Here is a more authentic southern porial, which traditionally uses coriander seeds, peppercorns, fennel and fenugreek seeds in its spice mixture. It is quite hot as well, and quite delicious.

Serves 4–6

1 tablespoon coriander seeds

1 teaspoon black peppercorns

1 teaspoon fennel seeds

10 fenugreek seeds

4 cloves

4 dried hot red chillies

6 tablespoons olive or groundnut oil

2 onions, very finely chopped

1 teaspoon very finely grated fresh ginger

2 teaspoons crushed garlic

3–4 fresh hot green chillies, very finely chopped

900g (2lb) boneless lamb from the shoulder, cut into 2.5–4cm (1–1½ in) cubes

2 large tomatoes, very finely chopped

1½ teaspoons salt

400ml (14fl oz) tin coconut milk, well stirred

1 tablespoon finely chopped coriander, to garnish

Step one Put the coriander seeds, peppercorns, fennel seeds, fenugreek seeds, cloves and chillies into a small, cast-iron frying pan and set it over medium heat. Stir the spices over the heat until they are a shade darker and give off a roasted aroma. Transfer to a bowl and leave to cool, then grind in a clean spice grinder or coffee grinder.

Step two Pour the oil into a wide, non-stick pan, and set it over medium–high heat. When the oil is hot, add the onions and cook, stirring, until they turn brown at the edges. Add the ginger, garlic and green chillies and stir-fry for 20 seconds. Add the meat and cook, stirring, for 5 minutes. Stir in the tomatoes, ground roasted spices, salt and coconut milk and bring to the boil.

Step three Cover the pan, turn the heat to low and simmer gently for 1 hour or until the meat is tender. Uncover the pan and boil away a lot of the liquid, until a thick sauce clings to the meat. Garnish with finely chopped coriander to serve.

If you want to use pork, buy shoulder meat and cook it exactly like lamb. If you prefer beef, use good-quality stewing beef, add a little extra water and then cook it for 1½ hours or until tender.

Lamb with Spinach

This dish may be served with rice or bread. I think Fried Aubergine Slices (see page 136) and a yoghurt dish would also complement the meat well.

Step one Put the oil in a large pan and set over medium–high heat. When the oil is hot, put in the peppercorns, cloves, bay leaves and cardamom pods. Stir for a second. Now put in the onions, garlic and ginger. Stir-fry until the onions develop brown specks.

Step two Add the meat to the pan, along with the cumin, coriander, cayenne and 1 teaspoon of the salt. Stir-fry for a minute. Add 1 tablespoon of the beaten yoghurt and stir-fry for a further minute. Add tablespoons of the yoghurt in the same way until all the yoghurt has been incorporated. The meat should also have a slightly browned look.

Step three Add the spinach and the remaining 1 teaspoon salt to the pan, and stir to mix. Keep stirring and cooking until the spinach wilts completely. Cover tightly and simmer on low heat for about 1 hour 10 minutes or until the meat is tender.

Step four Remove the lid and add the garam masala. Increase the heat to medium. Stir and cook for a further 5 minutes or until most (but not all) the water in the spinach disappears and you have a thick, green sauce. Fish out the 2 bay leaves before serving.

This dish could also be made with beef. Use cubed stewing steak and cook it for about 2 hours or until it is tender.

Serves 6

8 tablespoons vegetable oil

¼ teaspoon black peppercorns

6–7 cloves

2 bay leaves

6 cardamom pods

175g (6oz) onions, finely chopped

6–8 garlic cloves, finely chopped

2.5cm (1in) cube fresh ginger, peeled and finely chopped

900g (2lb) boned lamb from the shoulder, cut into 2.5cm (1in) cubes

2 teaspoons ground cumin

1 teaspoon ground coriander

¼ –½ teaspoon cayenne pepper

2 teaspoons salt

5 tablespoons natural yoghurt, well beaten

900g (2lb) fresh spinach, trimmed, washed and finely chopped, or frozen spinach, thawed

¼ teaspoon garam masala

Royal Lamb with a Creamy Almond Sauce

There are many Indian dishes that were inspired, a few centuries ago, by dishes from other countries. Shahi korma – lamb cubes smothered in a rich almond and cream sauce – owes its ancestry to Persian food. This dish could be served with Plain or Spiced Basmati Rice (see pages 164 or 171) or with an Indian bread (naan, chapati or paratha).

Serves 4–6

8 garlic cloves

2.5cm (1in) cube fresh ginger, peeled and chopped

50g (2oz) blanched, slivered almonds

7 tablespoons vegetable oil

900g (2lb) boned lamb from the shoulder or leg, cut into 2.5cm (1in) cubes

10 cardamom pods

6 cloves

2.5cm (1in) stick cinnamon

200g (7oz) onions, finely chopped

1 teaspoon ground coriander

2 teaspoons ground cumin

½ teaspoon cayenne pepper

1¼ teaspoons salt

300ml (½ pint) single cream

¼ teaspoon garam masala

Step one Put the garlic, ginger, almonds and 6 tablespoons water into a blender and process to a paste.

Step two Put the oil in a wide, heavy non-stick pan and set over medium–high heat. When the oil is hot, put in just enough meat pieces so that they lie in a single uncrowded layer. Brown the meat pieces on all sides, then remove them with a slotted spoon and put them in a bowl. Brown all the meat this way.

Step three Put the cardamom pods, cloves and cinnamon into the hot oil in the pan. Within seconds the cloves will expand. Now add the onions and stir-fry until they turn a brownish colour. Reduce the heat to medium. Add the paste from the blender as well as the coriander, cumin and cayenne. Stir-fry for 3–4 minutes or until browned somewhat.

Step four Add the meat cubes to the pan, along with any liquid that might have accumulated in the meat bowl, the salt, the cream and 120ml (4fl oz) water. Bring to a boil. Cover, reduce the heat to low and simmer for 1 hour until the meat is tender. Stir frequently during cooking.

Step five Skim off any fat that floats to the top and fish out the cinnamon stick. Sprinkle in the garam masala and mix.

You could also make this recipe using 900g (2lb) stewing beef cut into 2.5cm (1in) cubes, but use 250ml (8fl oz) water in step four and simmer for 2 hours

Madras Fish Curry

You could choose from a variety of fish for this dish. Try thick, skinned fillets of mackerel, bluefish, haddock, sea bass or salmon, cut into 7.5cm (3in) chunks. You could also use kingfish or swordfish steaks, but ask your fishmonger to cut off the skin around them first and halve or quarter large steaks.

Step one Put the onion, garlic, ginger and vinegar in a blender or food processor and blend to a smooth paste.

Step two Put the oil into a large, wide non-stick pan over medium–high heat. When the oil is very hot, add the cumin, fennel and fenugreek seeds and let them sizzle for 5 seconds.

Step three Quickly pour in the paste from the blender, using a rubber spatula to get it all out. Stir-fry it for 10–15 minutes, until it is golden brown. Add the ground coriander, cumin and turmeric and stir for a minute.

Step four Add the tomatoes, cayenne, garam masala, salt and lots of black pepper. Cook, stirring, for another 2–3 minutes. Stir in the 200ml (7fl oz) water and bring to the boil. Cover the pan, reduce the heat to low and leave to simmer very gently for 30 minutes.

Step five Add the fish in a single layer. Allow it to simmer gently, spooning the sauce over the fish, until it has just cooked through.

Serves 4

1 onion, chopped

3–4 garlic cloves, chopped

2.5cm (1in) piece fresh ginger, peeled and chopped

2 tablespoons red wine vinegar

4 tablespoons olive or groundnut oil

¼ teaspoon cumin seeds

¼ teaspoon fennel seeds

12 fenugreek seeds

½ teaspoon ground coriander

½ teaspoon ground cumin

¼ teaspoon ground turmeric

2 tinned plum tomatoes, finely chopped

½ teaspoon cayenne pepper

1 teaspoon garam masala

¾–1 teaspoon salt

freshly ground black pepper

675g (1½lb) fish (see above)

KITCHEN TABLE

For a video masterclass on filleting salmon, go to www.mykitchentable.co.uk/videos/filleting

Goan Prawn Curry

One of India's favourite curries, this is also very simple to prepare. Be sure to use good-quality prawns. You could make an equally popular Goan fish curry using this recipe. Just replace the prawns with a large, thick fillet of haddock or salmon, cut into 4cm (1½in) cubes. Serve this dish with plain rice.

Serves 4

1 teaspoon cayenne pepper

1 tablespoon red paprika

¼ teaspoon ground turmeric

2 tablespoons ground coriander

1 teaspoon ground cumin

1 tablespoon lemon juice

¾ teaspoon salt, or to taste

3 tablespoons olive or groundnut oil

½ teaspoon brown mustard seeds

1 large shallot, cut into fine slivers

3 garlic cloves, cut into fine slivers

400ml (14fl oz) tin coconut milk, well stirred

450g (1lb) medium-sized raw prawns, peeled, de-veined, rinsed and patted dry

Step one Put the cayenne, paprika, turmeric, coriander, cumin, lemon juice, salt and 100ml (3½fl oz) water in a bowl. Mix well to form a smooth paste and set aside. You can prepare this paste in advance of cooking the curry.

Step two Put the oil into a large, deep frying pan and set it over medium–high heat. When the oil is very hot, put in the mustard seeds. As soon as they begin to pop – a matter of seconds – add the shallot and garlic. Cook, stirring, until they are golden brown. Stir in the spice paste and bring to a simmer. Turn the heat to medium–low, then cover and simmer gently for 10 minutes.

Step three Add the coconut milk and prawns and bring to a simmer over medium–high heat. Once the sauce is bubbling, turn the heat to low and simmer, uncovered, until the prawns have just turned opaque. Serve immediately.

Goan Clams (or Mussels)

In Goa this dish is served with rice. The rice absorbs the briny, garlicky, coconut-sweet, pungent-with-chilli juices, and the clams, mussels, or even cockles, go a long way. I like to serve this dish in a large soup plate with crusty bread on the side. The bread absorbs the juices, performing the same function as the rice.

Step one Scrub the clams or mussels well under cold running water with a plastic scrubbing brush, discarding any with open shells that do not close when tapped on the work surface. If you are using mussels, be sure to remove their trailing beards.

Step two Put the oil in a large wide pan and set it over medium–high heat. When the oil is hot, put in the onion. Cook, stirring, until golden brown. Add the garlic, ginger and chillies and stir for another minute. Then add the cumin, turmeric and salt. Stir for 30 seconds.

Step three Add the coconut milk and bring to the boil. Put in the clams or mussels, stir and return to the boil. Cover the pan tightly (with foil and the lid if necessary), and cook for 5–7 minutes over medium heat, until the shells open. Discard any unopened shells and serve immediately.

Serves 4

24 fresh clams or mussels

4 tablespoons olive oil

1 large onion, very finely chopped

7 garlic cloves, crushed to a pulp

2 teaspoons very finely grated fresh ginger

2–3 fresh hot green chillies, finely chopped (do not remove the seeds)

2 teaspoons ground cumin

⅓ teaspoon ground turmeric

½ teaspoon salt

400g (14oz) tin coconut milk, well stirred

Fish Stew

This simple and delicious dish may be made with kingfish steaks, cod steaks or chunky pieces of halibut or haddock fillets. In Kerala, this sauced dish is always served with rice, but you may serve it with boiled potatoes and a salad.

Serves 4

1 teaspoon salt, or more, to taste

½ teaspoon ground turmeric

450g (1lb) fish steaks or fillets, cut into 5cm (2in) cubes

4 tablespoons coconut oil, or any other vegetable oil

1 red onion, finely sliced

6 fresh hot green chillies, finely sliced

2.5cm (1in) cube fresh ginger, peeled and finely shredded

about 30 fresh curry leaves, if available

200ml (7fl oz) tinned coconut milk, well stirred, or thick fresh milk

2 tablespoons lime juice

Step one Mix together ¼ teaspoon of the salt and ¼ teaspoon of the turmeric. Rub over the fish. Set aside.

Step two Heat the oil in a large, wide non-stick pan or wok over medium heat. When the oil is hot, put in the onion, chillies and ginger. Stir once or twice, then add the curry leaves. Stir-fry for 3–4 minutes until the onion is soft.

Step three Add ¼ teaspoon ground turmeric to the pan, along with 150ml (¼ pint) water, and mix well. Bring to the boil and add the prepared fish. Spoon the sauce over the fish, add ¾ teaspoon salt and reduce the heat. Cover and simmer for 4–5 minutes, spooning the sauce over the fish and shaking the pan gently every now and then to prevent sticking.

Step four Add the coconut milk and shake the pan. Taste to check the salt, adding more if needed. Cover and simmer for a further 3–4 minutes, shaking the pan now and then. Add the lime juice, shake the pan gently and remove from the heat.

Pork with Calves' Liver and Chickpeas

This is an easy stew, hearty, nourishing and comforting all at once. It is, quite clearly, of Mediterranean origin. It may be eaten with a salad and also, if you like, with rice. I use the meat from 3–4 thin pork loin chops for this dish. It may be made in advance and reheated.

Step one Peel the potates and cut them into 1–2cm (½–¾in) cubes. Put the cubes in a bowl and cover with water. Dust the liver lightly with salt and pepper and toss.

Step two Put the oil in a large non-stick frying pan over high heat. When the oil is hot, put in the calves' liver. Stir-fry until it has browned on the outside but is still soft and slightly rare inside. Remove the liver with a slotted spoon and set it aside.

Step three Put the garlic and onion into the same oil and stir-fry for 1 minute. Then add the diced pork and stir-fry for 3 minutes. Add the tomatoes and their liquid, and keep stirring and cooking on high heat for 1 minute, then cover, reduce the heat to low and simmer for 15 minutes.

Step four Drain the potatoes and add them to the pan. Also add the chickpeas, 1½ teaspoons salt, some black pepper, the paprika and 150ml (¼ pint) water. Stir and bring to a simmer. Cover and cook for 15–25 minutes, or until the potatoes and pork are tender.

Step five Add the liver to the pan, plus any juices that may have run out of it, and heat it through.

Serves 4

225g (8oz) potatoes

150g (5oz) calves' liver, cut into 1–2cm (½–¾in) cubes

salt and freshly ground black pepper

4 tablespoons vegetable oil

3 garlic cloves, cut into fine slivers

1 onion, thinly sliced

350g (12oz) lean pork meat, cut into 1–2cm (½–¾in) cubes

275g (10oz) tinned tomatoes, lightly crushed

150g (5oz) tinned chickpeas

1 teaspoon paprika

Cod Steaks in a Spicy Tomato Sauce

I like to serve this with Rice and Peas (see page 175).

Serves 4

4 cod steaks, about
950g (2lb) in total

1¼ teaspoons salt

½ teaspoon
cayenne pepper

½ teaspoon
ground turmeric

9 tablespoons
vegetable oil

1 teaspoon
fennel seeds

1 teaspoon
mustard seeds

175g (6oz) onions,
finely chopped

2 garlic cloves,
finely chopped

2 teaspoons
ground cumin

1 x 400g (14oz) tin
chopped tomatoes

½ teaspoon ground,
roasted cumin
seeds, (optional)

½ teaspoon
garam masala

Step one Pat the fish steaks dry with kitchen paper. Mix together ¼ teaspoon of the salt, ¼ teaspoon of the cayenne and the turmeric and rub over the fish on both sides. Set aside for 30 minutes.

Step two Put 4 tablespoons of the oil in a saucepan and set over medium heat. When the oil is hot, put in the fennel seeds and mustard seeds. As soon as the mustard seeds begin to pop – in just a few seconds – add the onions and garlic. Stir-fry until the onions turn slightly brown.

Step three Add the cumin to the pan, along with 1 teaspoon salt and ¼ teaspoon cayenne. Stir once and put in the tomatoes and their liquid, the ground, roasted cumin seeds, if using, and the garam masala. Bring to the boil. Cover, reduce the heat to low, and simmer gently for 15 minutes. Meanwhile, preheat the oven to 180°C/350°F/gas 4.

Step four Put the remaining 5 tablespoons of the oil in a large, non-stick frying pan set over medium–high heat. When the oil is hot, put in the fish steaks and brown on both sides. Do not cook the fish through. Put the steaks in a baking dish. Pour the cooked tomato sauce over the fish and bake, uncovered, for 15 minutes or until the fish is done.

Haddock Baked in a Yoghurt Sauce

This is one of my favourite fish dishes – and it is so easy to put together. All you have to do is combine the ingredients in a baking dish and bake for about 30 minutes. You do have to boil down the sauce later but that takes just an additional 5 minutes. I like to serve this dish with Mushroom Pullao (see page 172) and Frozen Spinach with Potatoes (see page 132).

Preheat the oven to 190°C/375°F/gas 5. Cut the onions into 3mm (⅛in) thick slices and line a large baking dish with them. The dish should be large enough to hold the fish in a single layer, but need not be more than 4cm (1½in) deep. Cut the fish fillets, crossways, into 7.5cm (3in) long segments and lay them over the onions.

Put the yoghurt into a bowl and beat it lightly. Add the lemon juice, sugar, salt, black pepper, cumin, ground coriander, garam masala, cayenne and ginger. Mix well. Add the oil and mix again. Pour this sauce over the fish, making sure some of it goes under the pieces. Cover with aluminium foil and bake in the upper third of the oven for 30 minutes or until the fish is just done.

Carefully pour out all the liquid from the baking dish into a small saucepan. (Keep the fish covered and in a warm place.) The sauce will look thin and separated. Bring it to the boil. Boil rapidly until there is about 350ml (12fl oz) remaining. Take the saucepan off the heat, put in the butter and beat in with a fork. As soon as the butter has melted, pour the sauce over the fish. Garnish with fresh coriander sprigs to serve.

If you cannot get haddock, use any other thick-cut fish such as cod or halibut.

Serves 4–6

Grilled or Bhuna Fish Steaks

This is a simple and lovely dish to make for guests or for the family. It is light, full of flavour and cooks quickly. I often serve it just with new potatoes and green beans. On days when I have a little more time I make Stir-fried Cauliflower with Green Chillies (see page 127) and Potatoes with Cumin (see page 163) instead.

Serves 2–4

for the marinade

2 teaspoons finely grated fresh ginger

3 garlic cloves, crushed

1 teaspoon garam masala

½ teaspoon ground cumin

¼ teaspoon ground turmeric

½ teaspoon mustard powder

¼–½ teaspoon cayenne pepper

2 tablespoons lemon juice

½ teaspoon salt, or to taste

freshly ground black pepper

to cook the fish

5 tablespoons melted butter or olive oil or a mixture of the two

675g/1½lb fish steaks (or thick, skinless fish fillets), such as halibut, haddock, tuna, salmon or swordfish

Step one Combine all the ingredients for the marinade in a bowl, adding a tablespoon or so of warm water to make a very thick paste.

Step two Line the rack of the grill pan with foil. Brush it with 1 tablespoon of the oil or butter and place the fish steaks on top. Smother the fish on both sides with the marinade and set aside for about 15 minutes (no longer than 30 minutes). Meanwhile, preheat the grill to high.

Step three Drizzle half the remaining butter or oil over the fish and grill for about 5–6 minutes or until nicely browned. Turn the pieces over carefully, drizzle with the remaining butter or oil and brown the second side. Check the thickest part of the fish to see if it is cooked through. If not, turn off the grill but let the fish sit under it until it is done.

Indian mackerel seem to me to be much plumper than their English counterparts. Perhaps the warmer waters make them lazier. Goan fishermen on India's west coast roast them right on the beach over smouldering rice straws. The blackened skin is then peeled away and the now pristine, skinless fish is served with a simple vinegar dressing. A good fresh mackerel needs nothing more. Further up the same coast, in large cities like Bombay, the fish is marinated first in a dressing of lemon juice and fresh coriander and then fried or grilled. Here is the Bombay recipe. I often serve it with Mushroom Pullao (see page 172) and Cabbage with Peas (see page 148).

Cut the heads off the mackerel. Split them all the way down the stomach and then lay them out flat, skin-side up, on a firm surface. Now bone the fish this way: Press down firmly with the heel of your hand all along the backbone. This should loosen the bone from the flesh somewhat. Now turn the fish over so the skin side is down. Work your fingers (or else use a knife) under the bones to prise them away from the fish. Cut 2–3 shallow diagonal slashes on the skin side of each fish.

Serves 2

Combine the coriander, chilli, lemon juice, salt and black pepper in a bowl and mix well. Rub this mixture all over the fish. Set aside for 45 minutes.

Preheat the grill to high. Put the fish, skin-side up, in a grill pan with the rack removed, and dot with half the butter. Grill, 10cm (4in) away from the heat, for about 5 minutes. Turn the fish over, dot with the remaining butter and grill for 4 minutes or until golden brown and serve with wedges of fresh lemon.

to serve

Chicken Tikka with Tomato

As well as being a tasty light meal, this is quite perfect with drinks for a large party. Just stick wooden cocktail sticks into the chicken pieces and pass the tray around.

Serves 6–8

Step one Put all the ingredients except the chicken in a food processor or blender and process to a smooth paste to make the marinade.

Step two Cut the chicken breasts into strips 5cm (2in) long and 1cm (½in) wide. Put the chicken pieces in a bowl, add the marinade and stir to mix. Cover and chill for 1–5 hours.

Step three Preheat the grill to high and remove the rack from the grill pan. Line the grill pan with foil. Arrange about half the chicken on the foil in a single layer, leaving behind any marinade that does not cling to the meat. Grill the chicken for about 10 minutes or until there are light-brown spots on the surface. Turn over the chicken pieces and grill for another 10 minutes, until lightly speckled. Transfer to a warm plate, keep warm and cook the remaining chicken in the same way. Serve immediately, with wedges of lime.

to serve

For a video masterclass on marinating meat, go to
www.mykitchentable.co.uk/videos/marinatingmeat

KITCHEN
TABLE

Tandoori-style Chicken

Since I do not have a tandoor at home, I use my oven turned up to the highest temperature it can manage to make this dish. Also, I have given up painting my tandoori chicken red. It tastes just as good without the artificial colouring and is much healthier, besides. You can prepare this dish a day in advance by marinating the chicken overnight.

Cut each chicken leg into two pieces and each breast into four pieces. Make two deep slits crossways on the meaty parts of each leg and breast piece. The slits should not start at an edge and should be deep enough to reach the bone. Spread the chicken pieces out on two large platters. Sprinkle one side with half the salt and half the lemon juice and rub them in. Turn the pieces over and repeat on the second side. Set aside for 20 minutes.

Meanwhile, make the marinade. Combine the yoghurt, onion, garlic, ginger, chillies and garam masala in a blender or food processor and blend until smooth. Strain the paste through a coarse sieve into a large bowl, pushing through as much liquid as you can.

Put the chicken and all its accumulated juices into the bowl with the marinade. Rub the marinade into the slits in the meat, then cover and refrigerate for 8–24 hours.

Preheat the oven to its maximum temperature and set a shelf in the top third of the oven where it is hottest. Remove the chicken pieces from the marinade and spread them out in a single layer on a large, shallow baking tray. Bake for 20–25 minutes, until cooked through. Lift the chicken pieces out of their juices and serve with lime or lemon wedges.

Serves 4–6
for the chicken

for the marinade

to serve

Beef Baked with Yoghurt and Black Pepper

Ever since the Moguls came to India, there has been a method of cooking that Indians refer to as 'dum'. Meat (or rice) is partially cooked in a heavy pot covered over with a flat lid. The pot and lid are sealed with a very stiff dough. The pot is placed over a gentle fire and hot charcoals are spread over the lid. The meat cooks very slowly until it is tender, often in small amounts of liquid. So what I have done here is to update a very traditional Mogul recipe. Dum dishes do not have a lot of sauce. Ideally, whatever sauce there is should be thick and cling to the meat. The later Moguls, seduced by the chilli peppers brought over from the New World by the Portuguese, used them generously. I love to eat this meat dish with chapatis, parathas or naans. If you prefer rice, then the more moist pullaos, such as Mushroom Pullao (see page 172), would be perfect.

Serves 4–6

6 tablespoons vegetable oil

900g (2lb) boneless stewing beef from the neck and shoulder, cut into 4cm (1½in) cubes

225g (8oz) onions, very finely chopped

8 garlic cloves, very finely chopped

½ teaspoon ground ginger

¼–½ teaspoon cayenne pepper (optional)

1 tablespoon paprika

2 teaspoons salt

½ teaspoon very coarsely ground black pepper

300ml (½ pint) natural yoghurt, lightly beaten

Step one Preheat the oven to 180°C/350°F/gas 4. Put the oil in a wide, flameproof casserole and set over medium–high heat. When the oil is hot, put in as many meat pieces as the pan will hold easily in a single layer. Brown the meat pieces on all sides and set them aside in a deep plate. Brown all the meat this way.

Step two Add the onions and garlic to the pan and reduce the heat to medium. Stir-fry for about 10 minutes or until browned. Add the browned meat and any juices. Also add the ginger, cayenne, paprika, salt and black pepper and stir for a minute.

Step three Add the yoghurt to the pan and bring to a simmer. Cover tightly with foil and then with a lid, and bake for 1½ hours. If the meat is not tender after this time, pour in 150ml (¼ pint) boiling water, cover tightly and bake for a further 20–30 minutes or until the meat is tender. Stir gently before serving.

You could also make this dish with stewing lamb from the shoulder.

Lamb or Beef Kebabs

These kebabs make for an excellent hassle-free meal. You can prepare the meat a day in advance by marinating it overnight.

Put the meat pieces in a stainless-steel or other non-metallic bowl. In a separate bowl, combine all the marinade ingredients and mix well with a fork. Hold a sieve over the meat and pour the marinade into it. Push this mixture through the sieve, extracting all the paste that you can. Mix the meat and the marinade well. Cover and refrigerate for 6–24 hours.

Preheat the grill to high. Thread the meat onto skewers. Balance the skewers on the rim of a baking tin so all the meat juices drip into the tin. Brush the kebabs generously with oil and place the baking tin under the grill. When one side of the meat becomes lightly browned, turn the skewers to brown the opposite side, ensuring you brush this side first with more oil.

Serves 4
for the lamb

for the marinade

Easy Kebabs

When Indians and Pakistanis talk about their beloved kebabs, they are referring to a very large and varied family of dry (i.e., unsauced) meat dishes. Kebabs can be made, like hamburgers, out of minced raw meat (Chappali Kebab, for example) or patties could be made out of finely ground, cooked meat and fried (such as the Shami Kebab). If minced meat is wrapped around a skewer before grilling it might be called a Seekh Kebab. If chicken chunks are marinated, skewered and cooked in a tandoor, the dish would be Chicken Tikka, which is yet another type of kebab. Often, thin slices of meat are marinated with spices and nuts and then cooked on a hot griddle or stone, as in this recipe. You may make these with lamb or beef, cut into thin slices.

Serves 6–8

450g (1lb) tender
beef or lamb steak

2 teaspoons
very finely grated
fresh ginger

1 teaspoon
crushed garlic

¼ fresh hot green
chilli, very finely
chopped

1½ teaspoon
ground cumin

1 teaspoon
garam masala

¼ teaspoon salt

freshly ground
black pepper

about 1 tablespoon
olive oil

to serve

lime wedges

fresh mint sprigs

Step one Cut the meat across the grain into very thin, neat slices, about 7.5cm (3in) long and 2.5cm (1in) wide. Put them into a bowl.

Step two Add the ginger, garlic, chillies, cumin, garam masala, salt and lots of black pepper. Toss well to mix. Cover and set aside in the refrigerator for 2 hours or even overnight.

Step three Brush a heavy frying pan, preferably a cast-iron one, or a griddle with the oil and set it over high heat. When it is very hot, lay as many meat slices in it as will fit easily in a single layer. Do not overcrowd the pan. When the meat has browned underneath, turn the slices over to brown the second side. Transfer to a warm serving plate and keep warm while you cook the remaining meat. Serve with wedges of lime and sprigs of mint.

Turkey Kebabs

Kebabs can be made out of almost any meat. Turkey is easily available, and low in saturated fat, so I use it quite often. These kebabs are best served in pockets of pitta bread along with Fresh Coriander Chutney (see page 200), sliced onions and tomatoes and a squeeze of lemon, or wrapped in parathas. To serve with drinks make the patties much smaller.

Step one In a large bowl put the turkey, 4 tablespoons of the breadcrumbs and all the remaining ingredients except for the vegetable oil, the thin slices of tomato and onion to be used for the garnish and the lemon wedges. Mix well and form six 7.5cm (3in) patties.

Step two Put the remaining 8 tablespoons breadcrumbs on a plate and dip each patty in them. There should be a thin layer of crumbs on all sides. Cover and refrigerate the patties in a single layer until needed.

Step three Put enough oil in a large frying pan to cover the bottom lightly and set over medium–high heat. When the oil is hot, put in as many patties as the pan will hold easily in a single layer. Cook for 3 minutes on each side, reduce the heat to medium and cook for a further 2–3 minutes on each side. Cook the remaining patties in the same way. Garnish the patties with the thinly sliced tomato and onion and some chopped fresh coriander and eat the patties with generous squeezes of lemon juice.

Makes 6

450g (1lb) dark turkey meat, finely minced

12 tablespoons fine dry breadcrumbs

¾ teaspoon salt

¾ teaspoon garam masala

½ teaspoon cumin seeds

½ teaspoon coriander seeds

8 tablespoons finely chopped fresh coriander, plus a little extra to garnish

2–3 fresh hot green chillies, chopped

50g (2oz) onion, finely chopped, plus a little extra, finely sliced, to garnish

2 teaspoons finely grated fresh ginger

50g (2oz) finely chopped tomatoes, plus a little extra, finely sliced, to garnish

⅛–½ teaspoon cayenne pepper

vegetable oil, for frying

to serve

lemon wedges

Pork Chipolatas Cooked in an Indian Style

Indians cannot, of course, buy chipolatas in their local bazaars, but here is a simple Indian-style recipe that I use when I am rushed to get dinner on the table.

Serves 4

2.5cm (1in) cube fresh ginger, peeled and chopped

3 garlic cloves

225g (8oz) small courgettes

2 tablespoons vegetable oil

225g (8oz) pork chipolatas

100g (4oz) onions, chopped

1 teaspoon ground cumin

¼ teaspoon cayenne pepper

225g (8oz) tomatoes, peeled and finely chopped, or tinned tomatoes

½ teaspoon salt

Step one Put the ginger, garlic and 4 tablespoons water into a food processor or blender, and process to a paste. Quarter the courgettes lengthways, and then cut the strips into 4cm (1½in) lengths.

Step two Put the oil in a large frying pan and set over medium heat. When hot, put in the chipolatas and brown them on all sides. Put the chipolatas on a plate and set aside.

Step three Put the onions into the hot oil in the pan. Stir-fry until they begin to turn brown at the edges. Add the ginger–garlic paste and stir-fry for a minute. Add the cumin and cayenne, stir a few times and add the tomatoes. Stir for a minute. Add the courgettes and the salt. Bring to a simmer, cover, reduce the heat to low and cook for 10 minutes.

Step four Cut the chipolatas into three pieces each. Add them to the pan. Cover and cook for about 5 minutes or until the chipolatas have heated through.

Lamb or Beef Jhal Fraizi

Jhal Fraizi was a speciality of the Anglo–Indians in India. Often the Calcutta mixed-race community would have a very English meal of roast lamb or roast beef on Sunday, then transform the leftovers into a spicy Jhal Fraizi on Monday, thus paying culinary homage to both sides of their ancestry.

Step one Cut the cooked meat into slivers about 5mm (¼in) thick, 5mm (¼in) wide and 7.5cm (3in) long and set aside.

Step two Put the oil in a large frying pan and set it over medium–high heat. When the oil is very hot, put in the cumin, mustard seeds and fenugreek seeds.

Step three As soon as the mustard seeds begin to pop – a matter of seconds – put in the green pepper, chillies and onion. Stir-fry until the onion has browned and the mass of vegetables has reduced.

Step four Add the meat, Worcestershire sauce, ground cumin, coriander, turmeric, salt and pepper. Cook, stirring, over medium–high heat for 3–4 minutes, until the meat has heated through. Taste for balance of seasonings, adding more of whatever you need.

Serves 3–4

350g (12oz) cooked boneless roast lamb or beef

3 tablespoons olive or groundnut oil

¼ teaspoon cumin seeds

½ teaspoon brown mustard seeds

8 fenugreek seeds

100g (4oz) green peppers, seeded and cut lengthways into slivers 3mm (⅛in) thick

1–2 fresh hot green chillies, cut into long, thin slivers (do not remove the seeds)

150g (5oz) onion, cut into thin half rings

1 teaspoon Worcestershire sauce

1 teaspoon ground cumin

1 teaspoon ground coriander

¼ teaspoon ground turmeric

¾ teaspoon salt

freshly ground black pepper

Minced Meat with Peas

I associate this dish with very pleasurable family picnics that we had, sometimes in the private compartments of slightly sooty, steam-engined trains, and sometimes in the immaculate public gardens of historic Mogul palaces. The mince, invariably at room temperature, was eaten with pooris or parathas that had been stacked tightly in aluminium containers. There was always a pickle, to perk things up, and some kind of onion relish, too.

Serves 4–6

4 tablespoons vegetable oil

75g (3oz) onions, finely chopped

6–7 garlic cloves, finely chopped

750g (1¾lb) minced lamb, or minced beef

2.5cm (1in) cube fresh ginger, peeled and grated to a pulp

1–2 fresh hot green chillies, minced

1 teaspoon ground coriander

1 teaspoon ground cumin

¼ teaspoon cayenne pepper

175–200g (6–7oz) peas, either frozen and defrosted under warm running water, or fresh

4–6 heaped tablespoons chopped fresh coriander

1¼ teaspoons salt

1 teaspoon garam masala

1½ tablespoons lemon juice

Step one Put the oil in a wide, medium-sized pan and set over medium–high heat. When the oil is hot, put in the onions and stir-fry until they are lightly browned. Add the garlic. Stir-fry for a further minute. Now put in the mince, ginger, green chillies, ground coriander, cumin and cayenne. Stir-fry the meat for 5 minutes, breaking up lumps as you do so. Add 175ml (6fl oz) water and bring to a boil. Cover, reduce the heat to low, and simmer for 30 minutes.

Step two Add the peas to the pan, along with the fresh coriander, salt, garam masala, lemon juice and 120ml (4fl oz) water. Mix and bring to a simmer. Cover and cook on low heat for a further 10 minutes or until the peas are tender.

Step three Taste for seasonings and adjust the balance of salt and lemon juice if needed.

A lot of fat might have collected at the bottom of the pan, but do not serve this. When ready to serve, lift the mince and peas out of the fat with a slotted spoon.

Kashmiri Meatballs

These sausage-shaped meatballs taste very Kashmiri in their final blend of flavours. I often serve them with Plain Basmati Rice (see page 164), and a salad of carrots and onions.

Step one In a large bowl put the minced lamb, ginger, cumin, coriander, ground cloves, ground cinnamon, grated nutmeg, black pepper, cayenne, salt and 3 tablespoons of the yoghurt. Mix well. Wet your hands with cold water and form 24 long koftas – sausage shapes, about 6–7.5cm (2½–3in) long and 2.5cm (1in) thick.

Step two Heat the oil in a large non-stick, frying pan. When the oil is hot, put in the cinnamon stick, cardamom pods, bay leaves and cloves. Stir for a second. Now put in the koftas in a single layer and fry them on medium–high heat until they are lightly browned on all sides.

Step three Beat the remaining yoghurt into 250ml (8fl oz) warm water. Pour this over the koftas and bring to a boil. Cover, reduce the heat and simmer for about 30 minutes, turning the koftas around gently every 7–8 minutes. By the end of the 30 minutes no liquid other than the fat should be left in the frying pan. If necessary, turn up the heat to achieve this.

Step four Lift the koftas out of the fat with a slotted spoon. Leave the whole spices behind but use the bay leaves as a garnish, if you like.

Serves 6

900g (2lb) minced lamb

4 x 2.5cm (1½ x 1in) piece fresh ginger, peeled and finely grated

1 tablespoon ground cumin

1 tablespoon ground coriander

¼ teaspoon ground cloves

¼ teaspoon ground cinnamon

¼ teaspoon grated nutmeg

¼ teaspoon freshly ground black pepper

¼ teaspoon cayenne pepper

1¼ teaspoons salt

5 tablespoons natural yoghurt

7–8 tablespoons vegetable oil

5cm (2in) stick cinnamon

5–6 cardamom pods

2 bay leaves

5–6 cloves

Beef Patties with Coconut

The first time I had these patties was in Bali, as part of a banquet with Nasi Kuning, the festive yellow rice, at its centre. They can, of course, be served more simply with just a dipping sauce, along with some rice and a vegetable. The meat needs to be minced very finely, almost to a paste.

Makes 14 patties

for the patties

1 teaspoon
cumin seeds

1 teaspoon
coriander seeds

350g (12oz)
minced beef

100g (4oz) freshly
grated coconut

1 garlic clove,
mashed to a pulp

salt

lots of freshly ground
black pepper

2 tablespoons
plain flour

3 tablespoons
vegetable oil

for the dipping sauce

4 tablespoons
sweet soy sauce

4 tablespoons lime
or lemon juice

1 teaspoon salt

2–4 fresh hot red
or green bird's eye
chillies, finely sliced

3 tablespoons
roasted peanuts,
finely chopped

to serve

lime wedges

Step one To make the patties, put the cumin and coriander seeds into a small cast-iron frying pan over medium heat. Stir and dry-roast the seeds until they turn a shade darker and emit a roasted aroma. Then grind them in a clean coffee grinder or spice grinder.

Step two Put the meat into a food processor. Add the coconut, garlic, ¾ teaspoon salt, black pepper and the roasted cumin and coriander. Let the machine run until the meat becomes a coarse paste. Take the paste and form 14 balls about 4cm (1½in) round. Flatten the balls into 5cm (2in) patties. Put the flour on a plate, sprinkle salt and pepper over it, and dip each patty in the flour. Dust off excess flour.

Step three Heat the oil in a frying pan over medium–high heat. When the oil is hot, put in as many patties as the pan will hold easily and fry them for 3–4 minutes each side until they are browned and cooked through. Cook all the patties this way and keep warm.

Step four To make the sauce, mix together all the ingredients in a bowl, putting the peanuts in only just before serving. Mix well. Pass the sauce separately to spoon over the patties, along with a lime wedge to squeeze over the patties.

If you wish to use desiccated, unsweetened coconut instead of fresh coconut, mix 40g (1½ oz) with 120ml (4fl oz) very hot water and leave for 1 hour before mixing it with the meat.

Minced Lamb with Mint

This dish may be served with rice, a pulse and a yoghurt relish. I often use it to stuff tomatoes. Get firm, good-sized tomatoes and slice off a cap at the top. Scoop out the insides without breaking the skin and then season the inside of the tomato with salt and pepper. Stuff loosely with the mince, put the caps back on and bake in a 200°C/400°F/gas 6 oven for 15 minutes or until the skin begins to crinkle. Serve with rice and a salad.

Step one Chop half the onions finely and set aside. Chop the other half coarsely and put them, along with the garlic, ginger and 3 tablespoons water, into a blender. Process to a smooth paste. Empty into a small bowl, add the cumin, coriander, turmeric and cayenne, and mix.

Step two Put the oil in a 25cm (10in) frying pan and set over high heat. When the oil is hot, put in the cardamom pods and cloves. Two seconds later, put in the finely chopped onions. Stir-fry them until they turn fairly brown. Reduce the heat to medium and add the spice mixture. Stir-fry for 3–4 minutes. If the spice mixture sticks to the pan, sprinkle in a tablespoon of water and keep frying.

Step three Add the minced meat to the pan. Break up all the lumps and stir the mince about until it loses all its pinkness, then stir-fry for a further minute after that. Add the salt and mix. Cover, reduce the heat to very low and let the mince cook in its own juices for 25 minutes.

Step four Remove the cover and spoon off most of the accumulated fat. Add the chopped mint, garam masala and lemon juice. Stir to mix and bring to a simmer. Cover and simmer on very low heat for 3 minutes.

Serves 6

175g (6oz) onions

8–9 garlic cloves

5 x 2.5cm (2 x 1in) piece fresh ginger, peeled and chopped

2 tablespoons ground cumin

4 teaspoons ground coriander

1 teaspoon ground turmeric

¼–1 teaspoon cayenne pepper

4 tablespoons vegetable oil

4 cardamom pods

6 cloves

900g (2lb) minced lamb

1¼ teaspoons salt

50g (2oz) finely chopped fresh mint

¼ teaspoon garam masala

1½ tablespoons lemon juice

Beef or Lamb Chilli-fry

The Goans have borrowed most recently from the Chinese and this dish is now a new local delicacy, found in most of the thatched shacks along the beaches of Goa.

Serves 3–4

350g (12oz) tender
beefsteak or boned
lamb from the leg
or shoulder

175g (6oz) onions,
finely chopped

5 garlic cloves,
coarsely chopped

2.5cm (1in) piece fresh
ginger, peeled and
chopped

½ teaspoon
cayenne pepper

½ teaspoon
ground turmeric

1 teaspoon
ground coriander

1 teaspoon
ground cumin

¾ teaspoon salt,
or to taste

5 tablespoons
vegetable oil

3–4 fresh hot green
chillies, seeded and
cut into long strips

Step one Cut the meat into thin strips as you would for Chinese food. Put half the onion, the garlic and the ginger into a blender with 2–3 tablespoons water and process. Add the cayenne pepper, turmeric, coriander and cumin and process to a paste. Rub the beef with 2 teaspoons of this paste and ¼ teaspoon of the salt. Set aside for 10 minutes.

Step two Heat 2 tablespoons of the oil in a wok or large non-stick frying pan over high heat. When hot, put in the remaining onion. Stir-fry until lightly browned. Add the meat and stir-fry over very high heat until it begins to lose its raw look. Remove the meat and onion.

Step three Wipe out the wok or frying pan and put in the remaining 3 tablespoons of oil. Set over medium–high heat. When the oil is hot, add the chillies and stir-fry for a minute until lightly browned. Put in the remaining spice paste and stir-fry for about 5–6 minutes until it is lightly browned. Add the meat and onion, ½ teaspoon salt and 6 tablespoons water. Stir over high heat for 1–2 minutes. Taste to check the salt and add more if necessary.

Tamarind Fish

Hilsa, a beautiful silvery fish, is found in the estuaries of Bengal's rivers where it comes in from the sea to spawn. It is much loved and was the fish traditionally used in this recipe. Salmon makes a delicious substitute.

Serves 4

¾ teaspoon
ground turmeric

1 teaspoon salt

450g (1lb)
salmon steaks,
2.5cm (1in) thick

100ml (3½ fl oz)
mustard oil or any
other vegetable oil

3 tablespoons thick
tamarind paste

½ teaspoon
cayenne pepper

⅛ teaspoon sugar

½ teaspoon brown
mustard seeds

Step one Rub ½ teaspoon of the turmeric and ½ teaspoon of the salt over the salmon steaks. Set aside for 10 minutes.

Step two Heat the oil in a large, wide non-stick frying pan over medium–high heat. When the oil is hot, put in the fish. Fry each side for 2–3 minutes until golden. Remove the fish from the pan using a slotted spoon, leaving the oil behind. Set aside.

Step three Meanwhile, into a bowl put the tamarind paste, cayenne pepper, sugar, the remaining turmeric and salt, and 200ml (7fl oz) water. Mix well.

Step four Take 2 tablespoons of the oil used for frying the fish and heat it in a clean, large frying pan over medium–high heat. When the oil is hot, put in the mustard seeds. As soon as they pop (a matter of seconds), add the tamarind mixture. Bring to the boil. Reduce the heat to low and allow to simmer for 10–12 minutes, stirring regularly, until the oil bubbles at the surface and the sauce becomes very thick.

Step five Add the fish to the pan. Continue to simmer for 5–8 minutes, turning the fish pieces once very gently halfway through. The sauce should just coat the fish.

Calves' Liver in a Gingery Sauce

You may also make this with lambs' or goats' liver. For a quick lunch or dinner, serve this on toast with a green salad. The sauce can be made ahead of time. It is best to brown the liver and fold it into the sauce just before you eat.

Serves 3–4

for the sauce

5 garlic cloves

5cm (2in) piece fresh ginger, peeled and chopped

1–2 fresh hot green chillies, sliced

5 tablespoons vegetable oil

½ teaspoon cumin seeds

¼ teaspoon nigella seeds (kalonji)

125g (4½oz) onions, very finely chopped

6 tablespoons natural yoghurt

175g (6oz) tomatoes, finely chopped

¾ teaspoon salt

½ teaspoon garam masala

⅛ teaspoon cayenne pepper

for the liver

450g (1lb) calves' liver, cut into 1cm (½in) thick slices

salt and freshly ground black pepper

2 tablespoons finely chopped fresh coriander (optional)

Step one Place the garlic, ginger, chillies and 4 tablespoons water into a blender or food processor. Process to a paste.

Step two Put 4 tablespoons of the oil in a large frying pan and set over high heat. When the oil is hot, put in the cumin and nigella seeds. Ten seconds later, put in the onions. Stir-fry until the onions turn a reddish brown. Add the paste from the blender. Stir-fry it for 2–3 minutes. Put in 1 tablespoon of the yoghurt. Stir and cook until the yoghurt is incorporated into the sauce.

Step three Put in a second tablespoon of yoghurt and work into the sauce in the same way. Do this with all the yoghurt. Now put in the tomatoes. Stir and cook for a minute. Turn the heat down to medium. Stir and cook for another 5 minutes. Add the salt, garam masala and cayenne. Stir and cook for another 2 minutes. Add 175ml (6fl oz) water and bring to a simmer. Turn off the heat and leave the sauce in the pan.

Step four Before cooking, dry the liver pieces with kitchen paper. Sprinkle a little salt and lots of black pepper on both sides of the slices. Put the remaining 1 tablespoon oil into a clean non-stick frying pan set over high heat. When the oil is very hot, add the slices of liver in a single layer. As soon as one side has browned, turn over and brown the second side. Do not let the liver cook through and get hard. Remove the liver to a board and cut it into 1cm (½in) cubes. Set the heat under the sauce to medium. When the sauce is hot, put in the liver pieces and the fresh coriander, if using. Simmer for 1 minute, stirring once or twice, and serve.

Fried Plaice Fillets

This is one of the simpler fish dishes served in many parts of India, with each area using its own local fish. The breading is, of course, a Western influence. Wedges of lemon or some tomato ketchup may be served on the side.

Step one Cut the fish fillets, crossways and at a slight diagonal, into 2cm (¾in) wide strips. Lay the strips on a plate. In a bowl, mix together the salt, black pepper, cumin, turmeric, cayenne and fresh coriander or parsley. Sprinkle both sides of the fish and pat down the spices. Set aside for 15 minutes.

Step two Break the eggs into a deep plate. Add 4 teaspoons water and beat lightly. Spread the breadcrumbs on a plate. Dip the fish in the egg and then in the crumbs to coat evenly.

Step three Pour about 1cm (½in) oil into a large frying pan and set over medium heat. When the oil is hot, put in as many pieces of fish as the pan will hold easily. Fry for 2–3 minutes on each side or until golden-brown. Drain on kitchen paper and keep warm. Fry all the fish strips this way and serve hot.

Serves 4

675g (1½ lb) plaice fillets, dark skin removed

¾ teaspoon salt

freshly ground black pepper

1½ teaspoons ground cumin

½ teaspoon ground turmeric

½ teaspoon cayenne pepper

2 tablespoons very finely chopped fresh coriander or parsley

2 large eggs

175g (6oz) fresh breadcrumbs

vegetable oil, for shallow-frying

Fish in a Green Sauce

In my family, we often used to marinate chicken breasts in this sauce and then sauté them. The sauce is ideal for fish, too.

Serves 2–4

for the fish

2 fish steaks, about 675g (1½lb), skinned and halved or quartered

¼ teaspoon ground turmeric

¼ teaspoon cayenne pepper

salt and freshly ground black pepper

3 tablespoons olive or groundnut oil

for the green sauce

½ teaspoon brown mustard seeds

1 tablespoon finely chopped shallots

2 teaspoons very finely grated fresh ginger

3 garlic cloves, crushed to a pulp

1 large teacup finely chopped fresh coriander, plus whole sprigs to garnish

1 tomato, finely chopped

2–3 fresh green chillies, chopped

1 tablespoon lemon juice

about ¼ teaspoon salt

½ teaspoon garam masala

Step one Rub the fish all over with the turmeric, cayenne and some salt and pepper. Set aside for 15 minutes or longer (if longer, cover and refrigerate).

Step two Put the oil in a large, wide non-stick frying pan and set it over high heat. When the oil is hot, put in the pieces of fish and brown them briefly on both sides (do not let them cook through). Remove with a slotted fish slice and set aside.

Step three Put the mustard seeds into the oil remaining in the pan. As soon as the seeds begin to pop – a matter of seconds – add the shallots, ginger and garlic. Reduce the heat to medium–high and stir the seasonings until they are lightly browned. Stir in the coriander, tomato, green chillies, lemon juice, salt, garam masala and 150ml (¼ pint) water. Turn the heat to low, cover and simmer for 10 minutes. Return the fish to the pan. Spoon some of the sauce over it and bring to a simmer. Cover and cook gently for 10 minutes or until the fish is cooked through and serve garnished with coriander sprigs.

KITCHEN TABLE

Have you made this recipe? Tell us what you think at www.mykitchentable.co.uk/blog

Prawns in a Butter–tomato Sauce

Serve this elegant dish with plain rice. The sauce can be made ahead of time and refrigerated, but the stir-frying is best done just before serving.

Step one Combine all the ingredients for the sauce in a bowl and whisk until smooth. Cover and chill until needed.

Step two Peel and de-vein the prawns and then rinse and pat them dry. Chill, covered, until needed. Put the oil and butter in a large frying pan and set over high heat. When hot, put in the cumin seeds and let them sizzle for 10 seconds. Add the shallots and garlic and cook, stirring, until very lightly browned. Add the prawns, turmeric, coriander, cayenne and salt. Stir-fry until the prawns have just turned opaque.

Step three Pour in the sauce and heat it through, stirring as you go. Serve immediately.

Serves 4–5

for the sauce

1 tablespoon
tomato purée

¾ teaspoon salt

¼ teaspoon sugar

1 teaspoon
garam masala

½ teaspoon
ground cumin

½ teaspoon
cayenne pepper

1 tablespoon
lemon juice

200ml (7fl oz)
single cream

4 tablespoons water

for the prawns

550g (1¼ lb) raw prawns

2 tablespoons olive oil

25g (1oz)
unsalted butter

1 teaspoon
cumin seeds

2 tablespoons finely
chopped shallots

3 garlic cloves,
chopped

¼ teaspoon
ground turmeric

1 teaspoon
ground coriander

¼ teaspoon
cayenne pepper

½ teaspoon salt

Stir-fried Prawns with Mustard Seeds, Garlic and Mint

Prawns cook up so fast that I often use them for an easy meal. You need medium-sized raw prawns here, the kind sold without their heads. I like to serve this dish with plain rice and a simple vegetable or a salad.

Serves 3–4

4 tablespoons olive or groundnut oil

½ teaspoon brown mustard seeds

2 dried hot red chillies, each broken into 2–3 pieces

4 garlic cloves, finely chopped

450g (1lb) medium-sized raw prawns, peeled, de-veined, rinsed and patted dry

½ teaspoon salt

1 tablespoon finely chopped fresh mint

few squeezes lemon juice

Step one Put the oil in a large frying pan and set it over high heat. When the oil is very hot, put in the mustard seeds and red chillies. As soon as the mustard seeds start to pop – a matter of seconds – add the garlic and stir-fry for 3–4 seconds.

Step two Add the prawns and salt. Stir-fry until the prawns turn completely opaque.

Step three Stir in the mint and lemon juice to taste and serve immediately.

Tandoori-style Prawns

These marinated prawns are traditionally cooked in a tandoor. I cook them very quickly in a frying pan. You may easily double the recipe if you wish, just use a larger frying pan.

Step one To make the marinade, put the yoghurt into a bowl. Beat lightly with a fork or a whisk until it is smooth and creamy. Add the remaining marinade ingredients, stir to mix and set aside for 15 minutes.

Step two Push the marinade through a sieve into a clean bowl. Add the prawns and mix well, then set aside for 30 minutes.

Step three Remove the prawns from the marinade with a slotted spoon, leaving all the marinade behind in the bowl. Melt the butter in a 20–23cm (8–9in) frying pan over medium heat. When the butter has melted completely, increase the heat to medium–high and immediately pour in the marinade. Stir-fry for a few minutes or until the butter separates and you have a thick bubbly sauce clinging to the bottom of the pan.

Step four Add the prawns to the pan and fold them in. Cook for a few minutes, stirring gently. Do not overcook the prawns. Serve immediately.

Serves 2

for the marinade

4 tablespoons natural yoghurt

2.5cm (1in) cube fresh ginger, peeled and finely grated

1 large garlic clove, mashed to a pulp

5 teaspoons lemon juice

¼ teaspoon salt, or to taste

freshly ground black pepper

1½ teaspoons ground, roasted cumin seeds

½ teaspoon garam masala

2 teaspoons yellow food colouring mixed with 1 teaspoon red food colouring

for the prawns

225g (8oz) peeled, good-quality frozen prawns, defrosted and patted dry

50g (2oz) unsalted butter

Quick-fried Prawns

You could stick cocktail sticks in these prawns and pass them around with drinks, or serve them as a main course.

Serves 4

75g (3oz) rice
flour or cornflour

2 teaspoons
ground turmeric

1 tablespoon
cayenne pepper

2 tablespoons
ground cumin

2½ teaspoons salt

1 teaspoon freshly
ground black pepper

vegetable oil, for
deep-frying

350g (12oz) peeled,
good-quality frozen
prawns, defrosted
and patted dry

to serve

lemon wedges

Step one Mix together the flour, turmeric, cayenne, cumin, salt and black pepper. Pour about 4cm (1½in) oil into a deep frying pan set over medium heat. Meanwhile, dip the prawns in the flour mixture and coat them thoroughly.

Step two When the oil is hot, put in as many prawns as the pan will hold in a single layer. Fry until the prawns turn slightly crisp on the outside – just a minute or so – turning them around whenever you need to. Remove with a slotted spoon and drain on kitchen paper. Cook the remaining prawns in the same way. Serve them hot, with a little lemon juice squeezed over them.

This is quite a fiery dish. If you don't like your food too hot and spicy, you should substantially reduce the amount of cayenne pepper.

Prawns in a Dark Sauce

Serve this with Plain Basmati Rice (see page 164) and Tomato, Onion and Coriander Relish (see page 196).

Step one Put the onions, garlic and ginger in a blender with 3 tablespoons water and process to a paste.

Step two Put the oil in a 20–23cm (8–9in) wide pan and set over medium–high heat. When the oil is hot, put in the cinnamon, cardamom pods and bay leaves. Stir for 3–4 seconds, then add the paste from the blender. Stir-fry for about 5 minutes or until the paste turns a light brown colour. Add the cumin and ground coriander. Stir-fry for 30 seconds, then add the tomatoes and continue stir-frying until the paste has a nice reddish-brown look to it.

Step three Add 1 tablespoon of the yoghurt to the pan, and stir-fry for 10–15 seconds or until it is incorporated in the sauce. Add the remaining yoghurt in the same way. Add the turmeric and cayenne and stir for a minute. Add 300ml (½ pint) water, the salt and the prawns. Stir to mix, and bring to a boil. Stir and cook for about 5 minutes or until you have a thick sauce. Do not overcook the prawns.

Step four Sprinkle with the garam masala and mix. Remove the bay leaves and cinnamon stick Garnish with the chopped fresh coriander and serve.

Serves 4

75g (3oz) onions, coarsely chopped

5 garlic cloves

2.5cm (1in) cube fresh ginger, peeled and chopped

4 tablespoons vegetable oil

2.5cm (1in) stick cinnamon

6 cardamom pods

2 bay leaves

2 teaspoons ground cumin

1 teaspoon ground coriander

175g (6oz) tomatoes, skinned and very finely chopped

5 tablespoons natural yoghurt

½ teaspoon ground turmeric

¼–½ teaspoon cayenne pepper

¾ teaspoon salt

350g (12oz) peeled, good-quality frozen prawns, defrosted and patted dry

½ teaspoon garam masala

2 tablespoons finely chopped fresh coriander, to garnish

Prawns with Courgettes

We do not have courgettes in India but we do have a variety of similar squashes, which are often cooked with prawns and other seafood. Here is one such combination. I like to serve these prawns with Spiced Basmati Rice (see page 171) or Plain Basmati Rice (see page 164).

Serves 4

350g (12oz)
courgettes (see tip)

1¼ teaspoons salt

350g (12oz) peeled,
good-quality frozen
prawns, defrosted
and patted dry

5 tablespoons
vegetable oil

6 garlic cloves,
very finely chopped

75g (3oz) finely
chopped fresh
coriander, plus extra
to garnish

1 fresh hot green
chilli, finely chopped

½ teaspoon
ground turmeric

1½ teaspoons
ground cumin

¼ teaspoon
cayenne pepper

3 small tinned
tomatoes, finely
chopped, plus 120ml
(4fl oz) liquid from tin

1 teaspoon very finely
grated fresh ginger

1 tablespoon
lemon juice

Step one Cut the courgettes in four slices lengthways. Cut each slice, lengthways, into four long strips. Cut the strips crossways into thirds. Place the courgettes in a bowl and sprinkle with ¼ teaspoon salt. Toss to mix and set aside for 30–40 minutes. Drain the courgettes and pat dry.

Step two Put the oil in a wide pan or frying pan and set over medium–high heat. When the oil is hot, add the chopped garlic and stir-fry until the pieces turn a medium-brown colour. Add the courgettes, fresh coriander, green chilli, turmeric, cumin, cayenne, the tomatoes and their liquid, ginger, lemon juice and remaining 1 teaspoon salt. Stir to mix and bring to a simmer.

Step three Add the prawns to the pan and stir them in. Cover, reduce the heat to low and simmer for 3 minutes. Uncover, turn the heat to medium and boil away the liquid, if there is any, so that you are left with a thick sauce. Sprinkle with some fresh chopped coriander before serving.

I prefer to use relatively small courgettes, weighing about 100g (4oz) each. If you can get only larger ones, just cut them appropriately so that each piece is a little larger than a prawn.

Squid in a Spicy Spinach Sauce

These days you can buy frozen cleaned squid from most supermarkets and Chinese grocers. Serve this dish with plain rice or, as a refreshing change, serve it over pasta. You could substitute prawns or cubes of salmon fillet for the squid if you prefer.

Step one Cut the tubular body of the squid into 5mm (¼in) wide rings. Leave the tentacles whole or halved and chill, covered, until required.

Step two Put the oil in a large wide pan and set it over medium–high heat. When the oil is hot, put in the onion, garlic and ginger. Cook, stirring, until the onion has browned lightly. Add the turmeric, cumin, coriander, salt and some black pepper and stir for 10 seconds.

Step three Add the chillies, tomatoes and spinach and cook, stirring, for 3–4 minutes or until the spinach has wilted. Add 250ml (8fl oz) water and bring to the boil. Cover the pan and turn the heat to low. Let it simmer gently for 20 minutes, then blend the mixture coarsely, either with a hand-held blender in the pan or by whizzing it in a blender.

Step four Just before serving, bring the puréed spinach mixture to the boil. Drop in the squid and simmer gently for 3–4 minutes, until it is just cooked through.

Serves 4

550g (1¼lb)
prepared squid

3 tablespoons olive
or groundnut oil

1 onion, chopped

3 garlic cloves,
chopped

2.5cm (1in) cube fresh
ginger, peeled and
finely chopped

⅓ teaspoon
ground turmeric

1 teaspoon
ground cumin

1 teaspoon
ground coriander

1–1¼ teaspoons salt

freshly ground
black pepper

3–4 fresh hot green
chillies, chopped

150g (5oz) tinned
chopped tomatoes

225g (8oz) fresh
spinach, chopped

For a video masterclass on chopping vegetables, go to
www.mykitchentable.co.uk/videos/choppingvegetables

Squid with Coconut

Squid and cuttlefish of every conceivable size are common to the shores of Kerala and are eaten all along the coastline, although not further inland for some reason. Here is one of the many ways in which it can be cooked. Serve this dish with plain rice. It is quite hot, but deliciously so. If you wish to lessen the heat, just cut down on the cayenne pepper.

Serves 4

50g (2oz) freshly grated coconut

5 tablespoons coconut oil, or any other vegetable oil

1 red onion, finely chopped

1cm (½in) piece fresh ginger, peeled and finely chopped

about 40 fresh curry leaves, if available

1 tablespoon cayenne pepper

1 teaspoon ground turmeric

1 tablespoon ground coriander

450g (1lb) cleaned squid, sliced into 1cm (½in) wide rings

salt, to taste

25g (1oz) shallots, finely chopped

Step one Put the grated coconut into a blender. Add 100ml (3½fl oz) water and blend to a smooth paste. Set aside.

Step two Heat 4 tablespoons of the oil in a large, wide non-stick pan or wok over medium–high heat. When the oil is hot, add the onion, ginger and about 20 curry leaves. Stir-fry for 3–4 minutes until the onion is soft. Add the cayenne, turmeric and coriander and continue stir-frying for 2–3 minutes. Add the squid and some salt to taste and stir-fry for a further 2–3 minutes. Add the coconut paste, increase the heat and stir-fry for a further 5–7 minutes or until the squid is cooked.

Step three Heat the remaining oil in a small pan over medium heat. When the oil is hot, add the shallots and remaining curry leaves. Stir-fry until the shallots are golden.

Step four Add the shallot and curry leaf mixture to the squid, mix well and cook for a further 2 minutes. The sauce should coat the squid. Remove from the heat and serve.

If you wish to substitute unsweetened, desiccated coconut for fresh coconut use 25g (1oz). Barely cover with warm water and leave for 1 hour, then proceed with the recipe.

Stir-fried Cauliflower with Green Chillies

Here, rice grains are used as a spice. The secret of this dish lies in allowing the cauliflower pieces to brown. While it may be served with all Indian meals, I find that it goes equally well with a lamb or pork roast, with sausages and with grilled meats.

Step one Put the oil into a karhai or wok and set it over high heat. When the oil is hot, put in the rice and cumin seeds. Stir for a few seconds, until the rice is golden.

Step two Quickly add the cauliflower florets, ginger and chillies. Stir-fry for 5–7 minutes, until the cauliflower has browned a little.

Step three Add the salt, garam masala, turmeric and black pepper. Stir once and then add 4 tablespoons water. Cover the karhai or wok, reduce the heat to medium and cook for 2 minutes or until the cauliflower is just tender.

Serves 3–4

3 tablespoons olive or groundnut oil

1 teaspoon any raw rice

½ teaspoon cumin seeds

450g (1lb) cauliflower florets

2.5cm (1in) piece fresh ginger, peeled and cut into fine rounds and then into fine slivers

2 hot green chillies, cut into long slivers (do not remove the seeds)

¾ teaspoon salt

½ teaspoon garam masala

¼ teaspoon ground turmeric

freshly ground black pepper

Mushroom and Pea Curry

A quick-cooking dish and one of my party favourites, this may be served with rice or Indian breads, along with a dal and any flavourful meat dish. Use frozen peas when fresh ones are not in season.

Serves 4

4 tablespoons olive or groundnut oil

½ teaspoon cumin seeds

1 teaspoon finely chopped garlic

350g (12oz) medium-sized white mushrooms, quartered lengthways

2 teaspoons very finely grated fresh ginger

2–3 fresh hot green chillies, finely chopped

1 teaspoon ground coriander

1 teaspoon garam masala

1 tablespoon tomato purée

¾–1 teaspoon salt

150g (5oz) peas, either frozen and defrosted under warm running water, or fresh

2 tablespoons finely chopped fresh coriander

2 tablespoons soured cream

Step one Put the oil in a large non-stick frying pan and set it over high heat. When the oil is hot, put in the cumin seeds and let them sizzle for 10 seconds. Add the garlic, stir once and then add the mushrooms, ginger and chillies. Cook, stirring, until the mushrooms turn silken.

Step two Put in the ground coriander and garam masala and stir for 30 seconds. Then add the tomato purée, salt, peas, fresh coriander and 300ml (½ pint) water. Stir well and bring to the boil. Cover, turn the heat to low and simmer gently for 5 minutes.

Step three Stir in the soured cream and cook gently for another minute, then serve.

Instead of water you could use chicken stock in this recipe.

Moghlai Spinach with Browned Shallots

Moghlai recipes for vegetables are often quite simple but utterly delicious. Here, just a small amount of browned shallot slivers provides much of the flavour. To cut a shallot into slivers, first cut it lengthways into halves or quarters, going parallel to its flattest side (a lot will depend upon size, of course). Now cut lengthways again, into fine, long slivers.

Step one Wash the spinach and remove any large stalks. Then cut the spinach leaves into wide ribbons if they are large, or leave them whole if small.

Step two Put the oil in a karhai, wok or large frying pan and set it over high heat. When the oil is hot, put in the chillies and stir quickly once or twice until they darken. Immediately put in the slivers of shallot. Stir-fry over medium–high heat until they brown.

Step three Add the spinach, salt, sugar and garam masala. Stir well and cook until the spinach has wilted completely.

Step four Add the cream and cook, stirring, for 4–5 minutes, garnish with the dried red chilli and serve.

Serves 4

500g (1lb 2oz) spinach

3 tablespoons olive or groundnut oil

2 dried hot red chillies

25g (1oz) shallots, cut into fine slivers

½ teaspoon salt

½ teaspoon sugar

½ teaspoon garam masala

4 tablespoons single cream

1 large dried hot red chilli, to garnish

Frozen Spinach with Potatoes

In India, we combine potatoes with almost every grain, meat and vegetable. Here is one of my favourite recipes. It may be served with lamb or beef and an Indian bread or rice.

Serves 4–6

550g (1¼lb) frozen leaf spinach

100g (4oz) red onions

5 tablespoons vegetable oil

pinch of ground asafoetida (optional)

2 teaspoons black mustard seeds

2 garlic cloves, finely chopped

500g (1lb 2oz) potatoes, peeled and roughly cut into 2–2.5cm (¾–1in) cubes

¼ teaspoon cayenne pepper

1 teaspoon salt

Step one Bring the 300ml (½ pint) water to the boil in a pan. Add the frozen spinach, cover and cook until the spinach is just done. Drain in a colander and rinse under cold running water. Press out most of the liquid in the leaves (you do not have to be too thorough) and then chop them coarsely.

Step two Cut the onions into half, lengthways, and then crossways into very thin slices. Put the oil in a heavy-based pan on medium heat. When the oil is hot, put in the asafoetida, if using, and then, a second later, the mustard seeds. As soon as the seeds begin to pop – this takes just a few seconds – add the onions and garlic and stir-fry for 2 minutes. Add the potatoes and cayenne and stir-fry for a minute.

Step three Add the spinach, salt and 2 tablespoons water and bring to the boil. Cover tightly, reduce the heat to very low and cook gently for 40 minutes or until the potatoes are tender. Stir a few times during the cooking period, making sure that there is always a little liquid in the pan.

Peas in a Creamy Sauce

In this recipe frozen peas can be used to great advantage. The creamy sauce can be made a day in advance and kept in the fridge. This dish can be served with all Indian meals and it also goes well with lamb and pork roasts.

Step one In a bowl combine the sugar, cumin, garam masala, salt, chilli powder and tomato purée, then slowly, mixing as you go, add 2 tablespoons water. Slowly stir in the cream, then add the lemon juice, coriander and green chilli and mix it all well. Set aside.

Step two Heat the oil in a large frying pan and, when hot, add the cumin and mustard seeds. As soon as the mustard seeds begin to pop – this takes just a few seconds – add the peas and stir-fry for 30 seconds. Add the cream sauce and cook over high heat for 1½–2 minutes or until the sauce has thickened, stirring gently.

Serves 5–6

¼ teaspoon sugar

½ teaspoon ground cumin

½ teaspoon garam masala

¾ teaspoon salt

¼–½ teaspoon chilli powder

1 tablespoon tomato purée

175ml (6fl oz) single cream

1 tablespoon lemon juice

2 tablespoons chopped fresh coriander

1 fresh hot green chilli, finely chopped

3 tablespoons vegetable oil

½ teaspoon cumin seeds

½ teaspoon black or yellow mustard seeds

550g (1¼ lb) peas, either frozen and defrosted under warm running water, or fresh

Fried Aubergine Slices

This is one of the simplest ways of cooking aubergines in India. Ideally, the frying should be done at the very last minute and the melt-in-the-mouth slices served as soon as they come out of the hot oil. Sometimes I arrange these slices, like petals, around a roast leg of lamb. They can, of course, be served with any Indian meal. Leftover aubergine slices, if there are any, may be heated together with any leftover Indian-style meat the following day. The combination makes for a very good new dish.

Serves 4–6

1 medium aubergine (about 550g/1¼lb)

1 teaspoon salt

freshly ground black pepper

½ teaspoon ground turmeric

¼–½ teaspoon cayenne pepper

vegetable oil, for shallow-frying

6–8 lemon wedges, to serve

Step one Cut the aubergine lengthways into quarters, and then cut, crossways, into 1cm (½in) thick wedges and set aside. In a small bowl, mix together the salt and pepper, turmeric and cayenne. Sprinkle this over the aubergine wedges and mix well.

Step two Put about 1cm (½in) oil in a 20–23cm (8–9in) frying pan and set over medium heat. When the oil is hot, put in as many aubergine slices as the pan will hold in a single layer. Fry until reddish-gold on one side. Turn the slices over and continue frying until similarly coloured. Remove with a slotted spoon and spread out on a plate lined with kitchen paper. Keep warm as you fry the rest of the aubergine slices.

Step three Cook the remaining aubergine in the same manner, adding more oil if needed. Serve with the lemon wedges.

Beetroot with Onions

I love beetroot, in almost any form. Even people who do not have a weakness for this particular root vegetable manage to succumb to the charms of this recipe. It is a kind of stew, thickened by the onions floating around in it, and somewhat tart in flavour because of the tomatoes it contains. As there is a fair amount of sauce, I frequently serve it with Beef Baked with Yoghurt and Black Pepper (see page 80), a somewhat dry dish, and with Tomato, Onion and Coriander Relish (see page 196). Chapatis are the ideal bread to serve with this meal, although plain rice would also taste good.

Serves 3–4

350g (12oz) beetroot (weight without stems and leaves), peeled

4 tablespoons vegetable oil

1 teaspoon cumin seeds

1 garlic clove, very finely chopped

100g (4oz) onions, coarsely chopped

1 teaspoon plain flour

¼–⅓ teaspoon cayenne pepper

225g (8oz) tomatoes, skinned and very finely chopped

1 teaspoon salt

Step one Cut the beetroot into wedges. For example, a medium-sized beetroot about 5cm (2in) in length, should be cut into six wedges.

Step two Put the oil in a medium-sized pan and set over medium heat. When the oil is hot, put in the cumin seeds and let them sizzle for 5 seconds. Add the garlic and stir-fry until the pieces turn golden. Add the onions and stir-fry for 2 minutes. Add the flour and cayenne and stir-fry for a minute. Now add the beetroot, the tomatoes, salt and 300ml (½ pint) water. Bring to a simmer, then cover, reduce the heat to low and simmer for 30 minutes or until the beetroot is tender.

Step three Uncover the pan, increase the heat to medium and continue to cook, uncovered, for about 7 minutes or until the sauce has thickened slightly.

This dish may be made ahead of time and reheated.

Cauliflower with Onion and Tomato

Here is a good all-round vegetable dish that goes well with most Indian meat dishes.

Serves 6

725g (1½lb) cauliflower florets

75g (3oz) onions, coarsely chopped

5cm (2in) piece fresh ginger, peeled and chopped

5 tablespoons vegetable oil

6 garlic cloves, very finely chopped

1 teaspoon ground cumin

1 teaspoon ground coriander

150–175g (5–6oz) tomatoes, peeled and finely chopped

½ teaspoon ground turmeric

¼–½ teaspoon cayenne pepper

½–1 fresh hot green chilli, finely chopped

1 tablespoon lemon juice

1¾ teaspoons salt

¼ teaspoon garam masala

Step one Soak the cauliflower florets in a bowl of water for 30 minutes. Then drain and set aside. Meanwhile, put the onions and ginger into a blender, along with 4 tablespoons water, and process to a paste.

Step two Heat the oil in a 23–25cm (9–10in) pan or deep frying pan and set over medium–high heat. Add the garlic and stir-fry until the pieces turn a medium-brown colour. Add the cauliflower and stir-fry for about 2 minutes or until the florets pick up a few brown spots. Remove the cauliflower with a slotted spoon and put in a bowl.

Step three Put the onion–ginger mixture into the same pan and stir-fry for a minute. Add the cumin, coriander and tomatoes and stir-fry until the mixture turns a medium-brown colour. If it starts to catch, reduce the heat slightly and sprinkle in a tablespoon of water. Continue frying until you have the right colour.

Step four Add the turmeric, cayenne, green chilli, lemon juice and salt to the pan. Give a few good stirs and reduce the heat to low. Add the cauliflower and any liquid in the bowl and stir gently to mix. Add 3 tablespoons of water, stir again and bring to a simmer. Cover and cook on gentle heat, stirring now and then, for 5–10 minutes or until the cauliflower is just cooked.

Step five Remove the lid from the pan and sprinkle garam masala over the dish. Stir to mix.

Black-eyed Beans with Mushrooms

I like this bean dish so much I often find myself eating it up with a spoon, all by itself. At a meal, I serve it with lamb, beef or chicken dishes, with rice or Indian breads served on the side.

Serves 6

Step one Put the beans and 1.2 litres (2 pints) water into a heavy-based pan and bring to the boil. Cover, reduce the heat to low and simmer gently for 2 minutes. Turn off the heat and let the pan sit, covered and undisturbed, for 1 hour.

Step two Put the oil in a frying pan and set over medium–high heat. When the oil is hot, put in the cumin seeds and the cinnamon stick and let them sizzle for 5–6 seconds. Add the onions and garlic and stir-fry until the onion pieces turn brown at the edges. Add the mushrooms and stir-fry until they wilt. Now add the tomatoes, ground coriander, cumin, turmeric and cayenne. Stir and cook for a minute. Cover, reduce the heat to low and let the mixture cook in its own juices for 10 minutes.

Step three Turn off the heat under the frying pan. Bring the beans to the boil again. Cover, turn the heat to low and simmer for 20–30 minutes or until the beans are tender.

Step four Add the mushroom mixture to the bean-and-water mixture and add salt, black pepper and fresh coriander or parsley. Stir to mix and bring to a simmer. Simmer, uncovered, on a medium–low heat for 30 minutes, stirring occasionally. Remove the cinnamon stick before serving.

225g (8oz) dried black-eyed beans, picked over, washed and drained

6 tablespoons vegetable oil

1 teaspoon cumin seeds

2.5cm (1in) stick cinnamon

150g (5oz) onions, chopped

4 garlic cloves, very finely chopped

225g (8oz) mushrooms, thickly sliced

400g (14oz) tomatoes, peeled and chopped

2 teaspoons ground coriander

1 teaspoon ground cumin

½ teaspoon ground turmeric

¼ teaspoon cayenne pepper

2 teaspoons salt

freshly ground black pepper

3 tablespoons chopped fresh coriander or parsley

Sweet and Sour Okra

This dish is an absolutely wonderful way to cook okra, also known as ladies' fingers or bhindi. It tastes best when made with young, tender pods. Okra are 4–13cm (1½–5 in) long, and both pods and seeds are eaten. Inside the pods is a sticky juice, which gives a rich, silky finish to dishes. When buying choose okra without any brown marks, which indicate they are past their best, and ones that snap easily without bending. Trim pods by cutting off the two ends. If the ridges are tough or damaged, scrape them carefully with a sharp knife.

Serves 4–6

7 medium
garlic cloves

1 dried hot red
chilli (use half if you
want a mild dish)

2 teaspoons
ground cumin

1 teaspoon
ground coriander

½ teaspoon ground
turmeric (see tip)

4 tablespoons
vegetable oil

1 teaspoon
cumin seeds

400g (14oz) okra,
trimmed and cut into
2.5cm (1in) lengths

1 teaspoon salt

1 teaspoon sugar

about 4 teaspoons
lemon juice

Step one Put the garlic and chilli in a blender with 3 tablespoons water and blend until smooth. Transfer to a bowl, add the ground cumin, coriander and turmeric, mix well and set aside.

Step two Heat the oil in a 23cm (9in) frying pan and, when hot, add the cumin seeds. As soon as they being to sizzle – this takes just a few seconds – reduce the heat and pour in the spice mixture. Stir-fry for 1 minute, then stir in the okra, salt, sugar, lemon juice and 4 tablespoons water. Bring to a gentle simmer, cover tightly and cook over low heat for 10 minutes or until the okra is tender. If you need to cook for longer you may need to add a little more water.

Turmeric is the spice that makes many Indian foods yellow. Apart from its mild, earthy flavour, it is used mainly because it is a digestive and antiseptic. Fresh turmeric is not unlike ginger, but is smaller in size and more delicate in appearance. Use fresh if you can. A 2.5cm (1in) piece is equal to about half a teaspoon of ground. Like ginger, it needs to be peeled and ground, which is best done with a little water in a blender. Use turmeric carefully as it can stain.

Spicy Green Beans

These green beans may, of course, be served with an Indian dinner, but they could perk up a simple meal of roast chicken or meatloaf as well. They are tart and hot and would complement the plainest of everyday foods with their zesty blend of flavours. Another good thing about them is that they may be made ahead of time and reheated.

Step one Cut the green beans crossways at 5mm (¼ in) intervals and set aside. Put the ginger and garlic into a blender or food processor. Add 120ml (4fl oz) water and process until fairly smooth.

Step two Put the oil in a wide, heavy-based pan and set over medium heat. When hot, put in the cumin seeds. Five seconds later, put in the crushed chilli. As soon as it darkens, pour in the ginger–garlic paste, stir and cook for about a minute. Put in the ground coriander and stir a few times, then stir in the chopped tomatoes and cook for about 2 minutes, mashing up the tomato pieces with the back of a slotted spoon as you do so. Add the beans, salt and 250ml (8fl oz) water. Bring to a simmer, then cover, reduce the heat to low and cook for 8–10 minutes or until the beans are tender.

Step three Uncover the pan and add the lemon juice, ground roasted cumin seeds and a generous amount of freshly ground black pepper. Turn heat up and boil away all of the liquid, stirring gently as you do so.

Serves 6

750g (1 ¾ lb) fresh green beans, trimmed

4 x 2.5cm (1½ x 1in) piece fresh ginger, peeled and chopped

10 garlic cloves

5 tablespoons vegetable oil

2 teaspoons cumin seeds

1 dried hot red chilli, lightly crushed in a mortar

2 teaspoons ground coriander

225g (8oz) tomatoes, peeled and finely chopped

about 1¼ teaspoons salt

3 tablespoons lemon juice, or to taste

1 teaspoon ground, roasted cumin seeds

freshly ground black pepper

For a video masterclass on using a pestle and mortar, go to
www.mykitchentable.co.uk/videos/pestlemortar

KITCHEN TABLE

Cabbage with Peas

Here is a simple cabbage dish that you could serve just as easily with grilled pork chops as with an Indian meal.

Serves 4

5 tablespoons
vegetable oil

2 teaspoons
cumin seeds

2 bay leaves

450–550g
(1–1¼ lb) green
cabbage, finely
shredded

150g (5oz) peas, either
frozen and defrosted
under warm running
water, or fresh

¼ teaspoon
ground turmeric

¼ teaspoon
cayenne pepper

1 fresh hot green chilli,
very finely chopped

¾ teaspoon salt

¾ teaspoon sugar

¼ teaspoon
garam masala

Step one Put the oil in a wide pan and set over medium–high heat. When hot, put in the cumin seeds and bay leaves. As soon as the bay leaves begin to take on colour – this just takes a few seconds – add the cabbage and peas and stir them about for 30 seconds. Stir in the turmeric and cayenne, cover, reduce the heat to low and cook for 5 minutes or until the vegetables are just tender.

Step two Stir in the green chilli, salt and sugar, cover and continue to cook on a low heat for a further 2–3 minutes. Remove the cover and sprinkle in the garam masala. Stir gently and mix. Remove the bay leaves before serving.

Gujerati-style Cabbage with Carrots

This is the kind of everyday dish that is served in the state of Gujerat. It may be served as well with roast lamb as with any Indian meal.

Step one Heat the oil in a wide flameproof casserole set over medium–high heat. Add the asafoetida, if using. A second later, put in the mustard seeds. As soon as the mustard seeds begin to pop – this takes just a few seconds – stir in the red chilli. It should turn dark red in seconds.

Step two Add the cabbage, carrots and green chilli, reduce the heat to medium and stir the vegetables around for half a minute. Add the salt, sugar and fresh coriander. Stir and cook for a further 5 minutes or until the vegetables are just cooked and retain some of their crispness.

Step three Add the lemon juice and stir to mix. Remove the whole red chilli before serving.

Serves 4–6

4 tablespoons vegetable oil

pinch of ground asafoetida (optional)

1 tablespoon black mustard seeds

1 dried hot red chilli

350g (12oz) green cabbage, finely shredded

350g (12oz) carrots, coarsely grated

½–1 fresh hot green chilli, cut into thin long strips

1¼ teaspoons salt

½ teaspoon sugar

4 heaped tablespoons chopped fresh coriander

1 tablespoon lemon juice

Sweetcorn and Potatoes with Mustard Seeds and Mint

In this dish the sweet, hot and sour flavours mingle to excellent effect.

Serves 4

150g (5oz) potatoes

175g (6oz) tomatoes

3 tablespoons vegetable oil

½ teaspoon black mustard seeds

¼ teaspoon cumin seeds

1 garlic clove, finely chopped

4 tablespoons very finely chopped fresh coriander

3 tablespoons very finely chopped fresh mint

1 fresh hot green chilli, finely chopped

sweetcorn kernels measured to the 450ml (15fl oz) level in a measuring jug

85ml (3fl oz) tinned coconut milk, well stirred, or water

½–¾ teaspoon salt

¼ teaspoon cayenne pepper, or to taste

1 tablespoon lemon juice

freshly ground black pepper

2 teaspoons ground, roasted cumin seeds

Step one First, boil the potatoes and, once they are cool enough to handle, cut them into 5mm (¼in) dice. Put the diced potatoes into a bowl and set them aside. Chop the tomatoes into 5mm (¼in) dice and put them into a bowl until needed.

Step two Put the oil in a large non-stick frying pan and set over medium–high heat. When the oil is hot, put in the mustard seeds and cumin seeds. As soon as the mustard seeds begin to pop – this takes just a few seconds – put in the garlic and potatoes and stir-fry until the potatoes are lightly browned.

Step three Add the diced tomatoes, coriander, mint and green chilli. Stir-fry for 1–2 minutes. Stir in the sweetcorn, add the coconut milk or water, salt, cayenne and lemon juice and bring to a simmer. Cover, reduce the heat to low and cook for 3–4 minutes or until the sweetcorn is cooked.

Step four Uncover the pan, add some black pepper and the ground, roasted cumin seeds. Stir to mix and taste for the balance of seasonings.

I like to make this in the summer when fresh sweetcorn is plentiful. I take the kernels off the fresh ears but you could use frozen sweetcorn just as easily. Let the kernels defrost a bit before you cook them.

Dry Okra

Sometimes, when I am in the mood for some really soothing, comforting food, I make Plain Basmati Rice (see page 164), Moong Dal and Red Lentils with Browned Onion (see page 180) and this okra, perhaps with a Tomato, Onion and Coriander Relish (see page 196) on the side. The okra does not have a sauce. It is just allowed to brown slowly and gently with cumin seeds and onions. Some ground, dry spices are sprinkled over the top towards the end. It is as simple as that, and so delicious.

Step one Wipe the okra pods with dampened kitchen paper, then pat dry. Cut off the conical top and the very tip of each pod and then cut the pods crossways into 1cm (½in) segments and set aside.

Step two Heat the oil in a large non-stick frying pan and set over medium–high heat. Put in the cumin seeds and let them sizzle for 10 seconds. Add the onions and okra, spreading the okra out evenly in the pan. Fry, stirring every now and then, for 10 minutes, spreading the okra out evenly in the pan each time you stir. The onions should begin to brown by this time.

Step three Reduce the heat to medium and continue to gently stir-fry in the same way for a further 5 minutes. Add the salt, ground cumin, ground coriander, amchoor or lemon juice and cayenne. Cook for a further 5 minutes, stirring or tossing gently as you do so.

Serves 3–4

450g (1lb) okra

8 tablespoons vegetable oil

½ teaspoon cumin seeds

175–200g (6–7oz) onions, coarsely chopped

½ teaspoon salt, or to taste

¼ teaspoon ground cumin

¼ teaspoon ground coriander

1 teaspoon ground amchoor or lemon juice

¼ teaspoon cayenne pepper

Tomato and Onion Cachumbar

A mini salad is served with almost every Indian meal. At its simplest, this can take the form of a sliced raw onion or wedges of cucumber.

Serves 4

1 medium onion, cut into 1cm (½ in) dice

2–3 medium tomatoes, cut into 1cm (½ in) dice

3 tablespoons finely chopped fresh coriander, plus a whole sprig to garnish

3 tablespoons lemon juice

1½ teaspoons salt, or to taste

¼ –½ teaspoon cayenne pepper (depending how hot you like it)

Step one Put all the ingredients in a bowl and mix well. Garnish with a coriander sprig and serve.

Potatoes with Sesame Seeds

Here is another of those easy, delicious dishes that you might enjoy both with Indian meals and with simple dinners of roast and grilled meats. I like the potatoes to have a few brown spots on them.

Step one Peel the boiled potatoes once they have cooled and dice them into 2cm (¾in) cubes. Heat the oil to very hot in a large non-stick 25–30cm (10–12in) frying pan over medium heat. Put in the cumin seeds, mustard seeds and sesame seeds. As soon as they begin to pop – this just takes a few seconds – put in the diced potatoes. Stir-fry the potatoes for about 5 minutes.

Step two Add the salt, cayenne and lemon juice. Stir-fry for a further 3–4 minutes.

Serves 6

900g (2lb)
potatoes, boiled
in their skins and
cooled for 3–4 hours

6 tablespoons
vegetable oil

2 teaspoons
cumin seeds

2 teaspoons black
mustard seeds

2 tablespoons
sesame seeds

about 2 teaspoons salt

¼–½ teaspoon
cayenne pepper

1 tablespoon
lemon juice

Dry Potatoes with Ginger and Garlic

Can you imagine cubes of potato encrusted with a spicy, crisply browned ginger–garlic paste? Add to that a hint of fennel, if you want it. That is what these potatoes taste like. You could serve them with an Indian meal of Minced Meat with Peas (see page 92), Indian bread and a yoghurt relish, or you could serve them with grilled or roast meats. It is best to make this dish in a large non-stick frying pan or a well-used cast-iron one.

Serves 4–5

625g (1lb 6oz) potatoes, boiled in their skins and cooled

5 x 2.5 x 2.5cm (2 x 1 x 1in) piece fresh ginger, peeled and chopped

3 garlic cloves

½ teaspoon ground turmeric

1 teaspoon salt

½ teaspoon cayenne pepper

5 tablespoons vegetable oil

1 teaspoon fennel seeds (optional)

Step one Peel the cooled potatoes and cut them into 2–2.5cm (¾–1in) dice. In a blender or food processor, blend together the ginger, garlic, 3 tablespoons water, turmeric, salt and cayenne until you have a paste.

Step two Put the oil into a large non-stick frying pan and set over medium heat. When hot, put in the fennel seeds if using. Let them sizzle for a few seconds, then add the ginger–garlic paste. Stir-fry for 2 minutes.

Step three Add the potatoes to the pan, and stir-fry over medium–high heat for 5–7 minutes or until the potatoes have a nice golden-brown crust on them.

Potatoes with Cumin

This is wonderful with Indian breads, yoghurt raitas and pickles. It may also be served with Western-style roasts.

Step one Cook the potatoes in boiling salted water until tender, then drain and leave to cool. Peel and cut them into 2cm (¾in) dice.

Step two Put the oil in a large non-stick frying pan and set it over medium–high heat. When it is very hot, put in the cumin seeds and fry for 10 seconds. Put in the potatoes, ginger, 1 teaspoon salt, ground cumin, cayenne and black pepper.

Step three Stir-fry the potatoes for 10 minutes, mashing them lightly with a spatula. Stir in the coriander and serve.

Serves 4

450g (1lb) potatoes, unpeeled

salt

3 tablespoons olive or groundnut oil

¼ teaspoon cumin seeds

2 teaspoons very finely grated fresh ginger

1 teaspoon ground cumin

½ teaspoon cayenne pepper

freshly ground black pepper

2 tablespoons finely chopped fresh coriander

Plain Basmati Rice

I was brought up with this fine-grained rice, which is a perfect accompaniment to many of the dishes in this book.

Serves 6

basmati rice measured to the 450ml (¾ pint) level in a measuring jug

¾ teaspoon salt

15g (½ oz) unsalted butter

Step one Pick over the rice for any grit, if necessary, and put it in a bowl. Wash it in several changes of water. Drain the rice and then pour 1.2 litres (2 pints) fresh water over the rice and let it soak for 30 minutes.

Step two Drain the rice thoroughly. In a heavy-based pan put the rice, salt, butter and 600ml (1 pint) fresh water and bring to the boil. Cover with a tight-fitting lid, reduce the heat to very low and cook for 20 minutes.

Step three Mix gently but quickly with a fork and replace the cover on the pan. Cook for a further 5–10 minutes or until the rice is tender.

South Indian-style Light, Fluffy Rice

In South India, rice is generally parboiled in a large, round-based, narrow-necked utensil, with lots of water. When it is almost cooked, a cloth is tied to the mouth of the utensil and all the water drained out. (This water is later given to the cows to drink.) The pan is tilted so it lies on its belly over very low heat. A few live coals are placed on top of it as well to dry out the rice grains. Here is how the same rice may be made in a modern kitchen.

Step one Preheat the oven to 150°C/300°F/gas 2. Wash the rice in several changes of water and leave it to drain.

Step two Pour 2.75 litres (5 pints) water into a large pan. Add the salt, if you wish, and bring to a rolling boil. Empty the rice into the boiling water in a steady stream, stirring as you do so. Let the water come to a boil again and boil rapidly for 7 minutes.

Step three Drain the rice in a large sieve, then quickly put the rice in an ovenproof pan. Lay the butter, if using, over the rice, cover tightly and put the pan in the oven for 35 minutes or until the rice is cooked. Mix gently before serving.

Serves 6

long-grain rice measured to the 450ml (¾ pint) level in a measuring jug

1 tablespoon salt (optional)

25–50g (1–2oz) unsalted butter (optional)

Aromatic Yellow Rice

You may use either basmati rice or American long-grain rice for this recipe. The yellow colour, here, comes from ground turmeric. I like to serve it with Chicken in a Red Sweet Pepper Sauce (see page 47).

Serves 6

long-grain or basmati rice measured to the 450ml (¾ pint) level in a measuring jug

1¼ teaspoons salt

¾ teaspoon ground turmeric

3–4 cloves

2.5cm (1in) stick cinnamon

3 bay leaves

3 tablespoons unsalted butter, cut into small pats

Step one Put the rice in a bowl and wash in several changes of water, then drain it. Pour 1.2 litres (2 pints) water over the rice and let it soak for 30 minutes.

Step two Drain the rice. In a heavy-based pan, put the drained rice, 600ml (1 pint) water, the salt, turmeric, cloves, cinnamon and bay leaves and bring to the boil. Cover with a tight-fitting lid, reduce the heat to very, very low and cook for 25 minutes.

Step three Let the pan rest, covered and undisturbed, for 10 minutes. Then add the small pats of butter, mixing them in very gently with a fork. Remove the bay leaves before serving but leave the cinnamon stick and the cloves in the rice as a garnish, if you like.

Spiced Basmati Rice

This is one of the finest – and most delicate – basmati rice dishes. It may be served with an Indian meal or with dishes such as roast lamb or grilled chicken.

Step one Pick over the rice for any grit, if necessary, and put in a bowl. Wash the rice in several changes of water and drain. Then pour 1.2 litres (2 pints) water over the rice and let it soak for 30 minutes.

Step two Leave the rice to drain in a sieve for 20 minutes. Meanwhile, put the oil in a heavy-based pan and set over medium heat. When the oil is hot, add the onion and stir-fry until the pieces have browned lightly.

Step three Add the rice, green chilli, garlic, garam masala and salt. Stir gently for 3–4 minutes until all the grains are coated with oil. If the rice begins to stick to the bottom of the pan, reduce the heat slightly. Add the chicken stock and bring to the boil. Cover with a very tight-fitting lid, reduce the heat to very, very low and cook for 25 minutes.

If you prefer, instead of cooking the rice on the hob you could put the pan, covered with the tight-fitting lid, in a preheated 160°C/325°F/gas 3 oven for 25 minutes.

Serves 6

basmati rice measured to the 450ml (¾ pint) level in a measuring jug

3 tablespoons vegetable oil

50g (2oz) onion, finely chopped

½ fresh hot green chilli, finely chopped

½ teaspoon very finely chopped garlic

½ teaspoon garam masala

1 teaspoon salt

600ml (1 pint) chicken stock

Mushroom Pullao

My mother used to make this dish with morel mushrooms. If you have some growing in your local woods, do, by all means, use them. Just slice them in half lengthways. You could also use the darker field mushrooms. In that case you would need to slice the caps. I tend to make this dish very frequently and find myself using the more easily available cultivated mushrooms. It is still a superb dish and may be served with almost any meat dish in this book. You could also serve it with a roast leg of lamb or with lamb chops.

Serves 6

long-grain rice measured to the 450ml (¾ pint) level in a measuring jug

150g (5oz) mushrooms

1 small onion

3 tablespoons vegetable oil

1 garlic clove, finely chopped

½ teaspoon finely grated fresh ginger

¼ teaspoon garam masala, plus extra to garnish

1 teaspoon salt

Step one Wash the rice in several changes of water and drain. Put the rice in a bowl. Add 1.2 litres (2 pints) water and soak for 30 minutes.

Step two Drain the rice well. Wipe the mushrooms with a dampened cloth or kitchen paper. Slice the mushrooms, from the caps down to the stems, into 3mm (⅛in) thick slices. Cut the onion into half, lengthways, and then crossways into very thin slices.

Step three Put the oil in a heavy-based pan and set over medium heat. When the oil is hot, put in the onion and garlic. Stir-fry for about 2 minutes or until the onion pieces begin to turn brown at the edges. Add the mushrooms and cook, stirring, for a further 2 minutes.

Step four Add the rice, ginger, garam masala and salt. Reduce the heat to medium–low and sauté the rice, stirring, for 2 minutes. Pour in 600ml (1 pint) water and bring to the boil. Cover very tightly, reduce the heat to very, very low and cook for 25 minutes.

Step five Turn off the heat and let the pan sit, covered and undisturbed, for another 5 minutes. Sprinkle with a pinch of garam masala just before serving.

Rice and Peas

This rice dish is flavoured, very mildly, with cumin seeds, making it suitable for almost any kind of meal.

Serves 6

Step one Wash the rice in several changes of water and drain. Put the rice in a large bowl. Add 1.2 litres (2 pints) water and soak for 30 minutes. Then drain and set aside.

Step two Heat the oil in a heavy-based pan set over medium heat. When hot, put in the cumin seeds and stir them about for 3 seconds. Add the onions and stir-fry until the pieces are flecked with brown spots. Add the peas, drained rice and salt. Stir and sauté gently for 3–4 minutes or until the peas and rice are coated with oil.

Step three Add 600ml (1 pint) water and bring to a boil. Cover very tightly, reduce the heat to very, very low and cook for 25 minutes.

Step four Turn off the heat and let the pan sit, covered and undisturbed, for 5 minutes. Stir gently before serving.

long-grain rice measured to the 450ml (¾ pint) level in a measuring jug

3 tablespoons vegetable oil

1 teaspoon cumin seeds

75g (3oz) onions, finely chopped

150–175g (5–6oz) peas, either frozen and defrosted under warm running water, or fresh

1 teaspoon salt

Tarka Dal

Here I have combined two different dals, but you could use 150g (5oz) of just one of them. Serve with Plain Basmati Rice (see page 164) or an Indian bread.

Serves 4

75g (3oz) yellow split peas (skinned mung dal)

75g (3oz) split red lentils (masoor dal)

½ teaspoon ground turmeric

1–1¼ teaspoons salt

3 tablespoons olive or groundnut oil

½ teaspoon cumin seeds

2 dried hot red chillies

1 garlic clove, lightly crushed but left whole, then peeled

Step one Put the two dals in a bowl and wash in several changes of water, then drain. Empty the dals into a heavy-based pan and add the turmeric and 900ml (1½ pints) water. Stir and bring to the boil. Quickly (before the pan can boil over) turn the heat down to low, then partly cover the pan and simmer gently for 40–45 minutes, until the dals are very soft. Stir in the salt, turn off the heat and cover the pan.

Step two Put the oil in a small frying pan and set it over medium–high heat. When the oil is very hot, put in the cumin seeds and chillies. As soon as the chillies darken – a matter of seconds – put in the garlic.

Step three When the garlic has browned lightly, lift up the frying pan with one hand and, with the other, take the lid off the dal pan. Pour the contents of the frying pan – oil and spices – over the dal and then put the lid back on for a few minutes to trap the aromas.

Green Lentils with Lemon Slices

I often serve this when I entertain. While it is perfect with Indian meals, I have also served it with a roast leg of lamb.

Step one Put the lentils and 750ml (1¼ pints) water in a heavy-based pan and bring to the boil. Partly cover the pan and cook for 40–45 minutes, until the lentils are very tender. Stir in the salt and fresh coriander, then turn off the heat. Now peel the lemon, removing all the white pith as well as the skin. Cut the lemon crossways into thin slices. Discard the small end slices and keep only the best eight of the large ones. Add them to the lentils and stir.

Step two Heat the oil in a small frying pan over medium–high heat. When the oil is very hot, put in the mustard seeds. As soon as they pop – a matter of seconds – put in the dried chillies. After a few seconds, when the chillies have darkened, add the garlic.

Step three Stir once or twice and then pour the contents of the frying pan over the lentils and serve.

Serves 4

175g (6oz) green lentils

¾ teaspoon salt

3 tablespoons finely chopped fresh coriander

1 lemon

3 tablespoons olive or groundnut oil

½ teaspoon brown mustard seeds

2 dried hot red chillies

2 garlic cloves, lightly crushed but left whole, then peeled

Moong Dal and Red Lentils with Browned Onion

Here two pulses are combined in an earthy, wholesome and utterly delicious preparation, one that I eat at least once or twice a week. I like to serve it with Plain Basmati Rice (see page 164) and any meat or vegetable dish.

Serves 6–8

175g (6oz) mung beans (moong dal)

175g (6oz) split red lentils (masoor dal)

½ teaspoon ground turmeric

1¼–1½ teaspoons salt

4 tablespoons vegetable oil or ghee

generous pinch of ground asafoetida

1 teaspoon cumin seeds

3–5 dried hot red chillies

1 small onion, cut into very thin half-rings

Step one Pick over the mung beans and red lentils for any grit. Combine them in a bowl and wash in several changes of water. Drain and put them in a heavy-based pan. Add 1.2 litres (2 pints) water and the turmeric. Stir and bring to a simmer (do not let it boil over). Cover with the lid very slightly ajar, reduce the heat to low and simmer gently for 40–50 minutes or until the pulses are tender. Stir a few times during the cooking.

Step two Add the salt to the mung beans and red lentils and mix. Leave, covered, on very low heat. Put the oil or ghee in a small frying pan and set over high heat. When the oil is hot, put in the asafoetida then, a second later, the cumin seeds. Let the cumin seeds sizzle for a few seconds, then add the red chillies. As soon as they turn dark red (this takes just a few seconds), add the onion. Stir-fry on medium–high heat until the onion turns quite brown and crisp. You may need to turn the heat down a bit towards the end to prevent burning.

Step three Pour the contents of the frying pan, oil as well as spices and onion, into the pulses and replace the cover on the pan immediately to trap the aromas.

Masoor Dal

Indians tend to eat protein-rich legumes with many everyday meals.

Step one Pick over the lentils for any grit. Place them in a bowl and wash in several changes of water. Drain the lentils and put them in a heavy-based pan with 1.2 litres (2 pints) water and the turmeric. Stir and bring to a simmer. Cover, leaving the lid slightly ajar. Cook the lentils over low heat for 35–40 minutes or until the lentils are tender, stirring occasionally.

Step two Add the salt to the lentils, mix and leave, covered, over low heat. Heat the ghee or vegetable oil in a frying pan over fairly high heat and, when hot, add the asafoetida followed by the cumin seeds. Let the cumin seeds sizzle for a few seconds and then add the chillies. As soon as they turn dark red – this takes just a few seconds – pour the contents of the frying pan into the lentils and mix.

Serves 6–8

350g (12oz) split red lentils (masoor dal)

½ teaspoon ground turmeric

1¼–1½ teaspoons salt

3 tablespoons ghee or vegetable oil

generous pinch of ground asafoetida

1 teaspoon cumin seeds

3–5 dried hot red chillies

Chickpea Flour Pancakes

This nutritious chickpea flour pancake may be served with all Indian meals just as bread might be. It can also be eaten at breakfast or as a snack with chutneys, pickles and other relishes.

Makes 5 pancakes

150g (5oz) chickpea (gram or besan) flour, sifted

½ teaspoon salt

½ teaspoon cayenne pepper

½ teaspoon ajwain seeds

1 small red onion, very finely chopped

5cm (2in) piece fresh ginger, peeled and very finely chopped

4 fresh hot green chillies, very finely chopped

5 garlic cloves, very finely chopped

2 tablespoons very finely chopped fresh coriander

about 3 tablespoons vegetable oil

Step one Put the flour into a large mixing bowl. Slowly add 250ml (8fl oz) water, mixing with a wooden spoon to make a smooth batter. Add the salt, cayenne, ajwain seeds, onion, ginger, chillies, garlic and coriander. Stir to mix and set aside for 15 minutes.

Step two Smear a large, wide non-stick frying pan with 1 teaspoon of the oil and set over medium–low heat. When very hot, stir the batter and pour about 4 tablespoons onto the centre of the pan. Quickly tilt the pan in all directions as you would for a pancake, spreading the batter to make about an 18cm (7in) pancake. Cover and cook for 3 minutes or until the pancake is reddish-brown at the bottom.

Step three Dribble another teaspoonful of oil around the edges of the pancake. Turn the pancake over and cook, uncovered, for a further minute or until golden. Remove from the heat and keep covered between two plates.

Step four Stir the batter and cook another pancake in the same way. Repeat the process until all the batter has been used up. Always remember to stir the batter before you use it.

Leftover batter may be covered, refrigerated and reused later.

Yoghurt Raita with Cucumber and Mint

Raitas are yoghurt relishes that can be made with fruit such as bananas and mangoes, with vegetables such as courgettes and cucumbers, with herbs like mint and coriander and with dumplings, nuts, and all manner of spices. They add both nutritional value and flavour to all Indian meals.

Step one Put the yoghurt in a bowl and beat lightly until smooth and creamy. Add the salt and cayenne and mix well.

Step two Fold in the grated cucumber and chopped mint. Garnish with a mint sprig and serve.

Serves 4–6

450ml (¾ pint) natural yoghurt

½–¾ teaspoon salt

¼ teaspoon cayenne pepper

10cm (4in) piece cucumber, peeled and grated

2 tablespoons finely chopped fresh mint, plus a whole sprig to garnish

Fresh Green Chutney

A very refreshing chutney, full of vitamins. I serve it with most Indian meals. You should also try it in a cheese sandwich (smear it on the bread instead of using butter).

Serves 6

6 tablespoons natural yoghurt

1 tablespoon lemon juice

1 tablespoon finely chopped fresh hot green chilli

2 heaped tablespoons finely chopped fresh mint

2 heaped tablespoons finely chopped fresh coriander, plus a whole sprig to garnish

$\frac{1}{3}$ teaspoon salt, or to taste

Step one Put 4 tablespoons of the yoghurt in a bowl and beat lightly until smooth and creamy.

Step two Put the lemon juice, remaining yoghurt, chilli, mint, coriander, and salt into a blender and blend until smooth. Empty this mixture into the bowl with the beaten yoghurt and mix well. Garnish with a coriander sprig and serve.

Yoghurt with Aubergines

This recipe offers a soothing, cooling and exceedingly simple way to serve aubergines.

Step one Put some water in the bottom part of a steamer to the boil. If you do not have a steamer, set a steaming trivet or a colander inside a large pan. Pour water into the pan in such a way that it stays just below the lowest part of the trivet or colander. Bring the water to the boil. Put the aubergine cubes into the steamer, cover and steam over high heat for 10 minutes. Ensure your boiling water does not dry out.

Step two While the aubergine is steaming, put the yoghurt into a bowl and beat it lightly with a fork or a whisk until smooth and creamy. Add the salt, black pepper, cayenne, if using, spring onion and chopped mint and mix with a fork.

Step three Lift out the steamed aubergine pieces and mash with a fork. Spread out the aubergine on a plate and leave to cool, otherwise the yoghurt will curdle when you add the aubergines to it. As soon as the steamed aubergine pieces have cooled, fold them into yoghurt and garnish with the mint leaves.

Serves 6

1 medium aubergine (about 550g/1¼ lb), peeled and cut into 2.5cm (1in) cubes

600ml (1 pint) natural yoghurt

¾ teaspoon salt, or to taste

freshly ground black pepper

⅛ teaspoon cayenne pepper (optional)

1 spring onion, cut into paper-thin rounds all the way along its length (including the green section)

1 tablespoon finely chopped fresh mint, plus a few extra mint leaves to garnish

Spicy Cucumber Wedges

These wedges are refreshing and deliciously crunchy and may be served with any Indian meal. It is best to prepare them at the last minute, just before you sit down to eat.

Serves 4

275g (10oz) cucumber, about 25cm (10in) long

$1/3$ teaspoon salt

$1/8$ teaspoon cayenne pepper

freshly ground black pepper

$1/3$ teaspoon ground, roasted cumin seeds

juice of $3/4$ lemon

Step one Peel the cucumber and cut it into half crossways. Cut each half into four lengthways. Arrange the wedges on a plate. Sprinkle the salt, cayenne, black pepper, ground roasted cumin seeds and lemon juice over them. Serve immediately.

Yoghurt with Walnuts and Fresh Coriander

Another cooling, nourishing dish. It may be eaten by itself or served with Indian meals.

Step one Put the yoghurt in a bowl. Beat lightly with a fork or a whisk until it is smooth and creamy.

Step two Add all the other ingredients. Stir to mix and serve.

Serves 6

600ml (1 pint) natural yoghurt

2 tablespoons finely chopped fresh coriander

½ fresh hot green chilli, very finely chopped

½ teaspoon salt, or to taste

freshly ground black pepper

1 spring onion, very finely sliced

65g (2½ oz) shelled walnuts, broken up, roughly, into 1cm (½ in) pieces

Apple, Peach and Apricot Chutney

This superb, sweet-and-sour chutney has the thick consistency of
a preserve and may be bottled and kept for long periods.

**Makes about 750ml
(1¼ pints)**

550g (1¼ lb) sour
cooking apples,
peeled, cored and
coarsely chopped

100g (4oz) dried
peaches, quartered

100g (4oz)
dried apricots

50g (2oz) sultanas

6 garlic cloves, peeled
and mashed to a pulp

two 2.5cm (1in)
cubes fresh ginger,
peeled and finely
grated

400ml (14fl oz)
white wine vinegar

400g (14oz)
caster sugar

2 teaspoons salt

½ teaspoon
cayenne pepper

Step one Combine all the ingredients in a heavy
stainless-steel or porcelain-lined pan and bring to a boil.
Turn heat to medium–low and cook, keeping up a fairly
vigorous simmer, for about 30 minutes or until you have a
thick, jam-like consistency. Stir frequently and turn the heat
down slightly when the chutney thickens as it could stick to
the bottom of
the pan.

Step two Let the chutney cool. It will thicken some more as it
cools. Pour into a clean jar and cover with a non-metallic lid.
Store in a cool place or keep in the refrigerator.

Gujerati Carrot Salad

This simple, lightly spiced, easy-to-make salad may be served with Indian meals – or with something as Western as grilled sausages. There are many variations to it, which you might like to try out on your family and friends. You could, for example, leave out the lemon juice, which highlights the natural sweetness of the carrots. Or you could add 2 tablespoons of sultanas that have been soaked in hot water for 2–3 hours ahead of time.

Step one In a bowl, toss the grated carrots with the salt.

Step two Put the oil in a very small pan and set over medium heat. When the oil is very hot, put in the mustard seeds. As soon as the mustard seeds begin to pop – this takes just a few seconds – pour the contents of the pan – oil and seeds – over the carrots.

Step three Add the lemon juice and toss. Serve at room temperature or cold.

Serves 4

350g (12oz) carrots, coarsely grated

¼ teaspoon salt

2 tablespoons vegetable oil

1 tablespoon black mustard seeds

2 teaspoons lemon juice

For more recipes from My Kitchen Table, sign up for our newsletter at
www.mykitchentable.co.uk/newsletter

Fresh Coriander Chutney

This is the kind of chutney that is made fresh in our homes every day. We eat small amounts – one or two teaspoons – with our meals, just as you might eat mustard with sausages. It also serves as an excellent dip for snacks such as samosas.

Serves 4–6

75g (3oz) fresh coriander leaves, coarsely chopped

½–1 fresh hot green chilli, coarsely chopped

1½ tablespoons lemon juice

½ teaspoon salt

½ teaspoon ground, roasted cumin seeds

freshly ground black pepper

Step one Combine all the ingredients in a blender. Blend, pushing down with a rubber spatula several times, until you have a paste.

Step two Empty the paste into a small glass or other non-metallic bowl to serve.

Spicy Matchstick Potato Crisps

This is a snack that Indians munch noisily while watching Indian movie epics where scantily clad girls shake their hips at the dashing heroes.

Step one Put the onions, garlic and red chilli into a blender or food processor and process to a paste. Empty the paste into a bowl. Add the cumin and coriander and mix them in.

Step two Cut the potatoes into slices 3mm (⅛in) thick, using a mandolin, food processor or knife. Stack about five slices together and cut them into 3mm (⅛in) wide matchsticks. You can either fry the potatoes as soon as they are cut, or else leave them to soak in water and pat them dry later for frying.

Step three Line a large plate with kitchen paper and set near the stove. Put about 1cm (½in) oil in a deep, 25–30cm (10–12in) frying pan set over medium heat. When the oil is hot, put in as many of the cut potatoes as the pan will hold easily without overcrowding. Stir-fry until the potatoes are golden and crisp. Remove the potatoes with a slotted spoon and spread them out on one area of the platter. Fry all the potatoes this way, spreading out each batch on the kitchen paper.

Step four Take the frying pan off the heat and remove all but 4 tablespoons of the oil. Put the frying pan back on medium heat and pour in the spice mixture from the bowl. Stir-fry until the mixture is brown and fairly dry. Take your time to do this, turning the heat down a bit if you think it is necessary.

Step five Add all the fried potatoes and the salt to the frying pan. Stir to mix, breaking up any lumps of spice as you do so. Drain again and serve.

Use more than one dried hot chilli if you want the potatoes to be more than mildly hot.

Serves 4–6 with drinks

100g (4oz) onions, coarsely chopped

2–3 garlic cloves

1 dried hot red chilli

1 teaspoon ground cumin

½ teaspoon ground coriander

450g (1lb) potatoes, peeled

vegetable oil for frying

½–1 teaspoon salt

Mango Lassi

This cool, smooth drink is a delicious thirst-quencher. You could use fat-free yoghurt, if you prefer. Out of season, use good-quality tinned Alphonso mango slices or purée instead of fresh mango.

Serves 2

250ml (8fl oz) natural yoghurt

150g (5oz) chopped, non-fibrous flesh from a peeled, ripe mango

2 tablespoons caster sugar

10 ice cubes

few drops of rose water (optional)

2 fresh mint sprigs, to garnish

Step one Combine all the ingredients except the mint in a blender and blend until smooth.

Step two Strain through a sieve, pushing through as much liquid as possible.

Step three Pour the lassi into two glasses. Decorate with the sprigs of mint and serve.

10 9 8 7 6 5 4 3 2 1

Published in 2011 by BBC Books, an imprint of Ebury Publishing. A Random House Group company.

Recipes © Madhur Jaffrey 2011
Book design © Woodlands Books Ltd 2011

All recipes contained in this book first appeared in Madhur Jaffrey's *Far Eastern Cookery* (1989), *A Taste of the Far East* (1993), *Indian Cookery* (1994), *Flavours of India* (1995), *Madhur Jaffrey Cooks Curries* (1996) and *Foolproof Indian Cookery* (2001).

Madhur Jaffrey has asserted her right to be identified as the author of this Work in accordance with the Copyright, Designs and Patents Act 1988

The Random House Group Limited
Reg. No. 954009

A CIP catalogue record for this book is available from the British Library

The Random House Group Limited supports the Forest Stewardship Council® (FSC®), the leading international forest certification organisation. All our titles that are printed on Greenpeace approved FSC® certified paper carry the FSC® logo. Our paper procurement policy can be found at www.randomhouse.co.uk/environment

Addresses for companies within the Random House Group can be found at www.randomhouse.co.uk

To buy books by your favourite authors and register for offers visit www.randomhouse.co.uk

Printed and bound in the UK by Butler, Tanner and Dennis Ltd
Colour origination by AltaImage

Commissioning Editor: Muna Reyal
Assistant Editor: Joe Cottington
Project Editor: Constance Novis
Designer: Lucy Stephens
Photographer: William Reavell © Woodlands Books Ltd 2011 (see also credits below)
Food Stylists: Katie Giovanni, Caroline Liddle and Marie-Ange Lapierre
Prop stylists: Cynthia Inions, Malika, Sue Rowlands and Helen Payne
Copy Editor: Marion Moisy
Production: Rebecca Jones

Photography on p4 © Muir Vidler; pages 6, 9, 10, 13, 14, 17, 18, 21, 26, 29, 30, 37, 53, 54, 58, 61, 62, 69, 73, 74, 77, 78, 85, 86, 90, 94, 109, 110, 113, 114, 122, 126, 129, 130, 137, 138, 142, 157, 162, 174, 177, 178, 181, 186, 189, 190, 193 and 205 © Jean Cazals; pages 42, 121, 154, 197 and 202 © James Murphy; pages 33, 34, 50 and 145 by Philip Webb © Woodlands Books Ltd 2011.

ISBN: 9781849903516